TO SEE THE ELEPHANT

TO SEE THE ELEPHANT

*The Civil War Letters
of
John A. McKee
(1861-1865)*

By
James R. James

Published by
LEATHERS PUBLISHING
4500 College Blvd.
Leawood, KS 66211
Phone: 1 / 888 / 888-7696

Copyright © 1998
Printed in the United States of America

ISBN: 1-890622-49-4

Library of Congress Catalog No. 98-67522

Illustrated by Col. Darrell L. Combs, USMC (Ret.)

Published by
LEATHERS PUBLISHING
4500 College Blvd.
Leawood, KS 66211
Phone: 1 / 888 / 888-7696

FOREWORD

IN ONE OF MANY LETTERS written to his brother during the Civil War, John A. McKee mentioned that he had secured permission from a superior officer to accompany a mounted raiding party in "hopes of seeing a little of the elephant." This nineteenth century slang meant that he wanted to be where the action was, and during the Civil War, in particular, it was the common soldier's reference to battle.

John Alexander McKee was the eldest son of Washington Joseph McKee and Sarah Jane Harper McKee. He was barely 19 when he enlisted in Company G, 44th Ohio Volunteer Infantry, on September 20, 1861. His brother James, three years his junior, remained at home with the family. It is quite apparent that the two boys had been close since it was to James that John wrote most of his letters. The letters that have survived the six score of years form the basic manuscript for this publication. Some letters were lost.

With the exception of the deletion of formal parts of the letters and some references to purely family matters, and except for correcting a few misspelled words (there weren't many), the letters are as John wrote them. While some of his conversations may seem a little exaggerated and others quite intimate, one should remember they were written by one brother to another.

I am grateful to Margaret S. McKee, a younger sister of John and James McKee, who preserved the family letters for many years until her death, and especially to their niece, the late Margaret Cummings of Topeka, Kansas, who made them available to me for research and publication.

JRJ

JOHN A. MCKEE
(44th Ohio Volunteer Infantry)
(8th Ohio Volunteer Cavalry)

1861

1861

EARLY IN THE AUTUMN OF 1861, the 44th Ohio Volunteer Infantry was organized at Camp Clark, located at the Clark County fairgrounds in Springfield. The people of Ohio were responding to President Lincoln's call on July 22, 1861, for 500,000 volunteers, following the defeat of Union forces at Manassas, Virginia (Bull Run). Regiments were being formed all over the state at the behest of Governor William Dennison.

Not all companies in the 44th were from Springfield, as several were recruited in surrounding counties including Darke County, the home of most of the members of Company G. John A. McKee enlisted as a corporal when the company was recruited at Greenville, the county seat located about seven miles from his home at Gettysburg.

Newspaper accounts indicate some difficulty in finding a regimental commander, but finally on October 15th, Governor Dennison appointed Samuel Augustus Gilbert, a former lieutenant colonel in the 24th Ohio, to head the regiment.

On September 16, 1861, the *Springfield Republic* announced that a promise had been procured from Senator Andrew Johnson of Tennessee to make an address during the coming fair in support of the "War for the Union" and suggested that the word be spread abroad in order to give a magnificent greeting.

On Saturday morning, October 5th, Senator Johnson arrived on the Little Miami train and during the day was greeted by thousands who braved the terrible rainstorms which occurred intermittently. When he spoke at the fairgrounds, his speech was reported as being "strikingly affecting throughout, at times brought tears to manly eyes and again thrilled all hearts with high resolve to do or die for our country."[1] Two days later, John McKee wrote his first letter to his brother James.

Camp Clark, Ohio
October 7, 1861

We had a pretty good time last week on account of the fair which was held on the same grounds we occupy, there being only a guard line between us, although we were only allowed to go over two or three times. I have had very good health since I came down here except a slight cough that I have had for a few days.

Andy Johnson spoke on the fairgrounds last Saturday. The whole regiment was called out to escort him from town to the fairgrounds. We formed in line and marched over to town through a drenching rain. When we got there, there was no Andy Johnson there, so you see we had the satisfaction of marching back through the mud and rain without seeing him. However, when we got back, we found him on the grounds. He spoke about two and one-half hours and made about the best speech I ever heard. While he was speaking, a Democrat came up and said that he, Johnson, was a G-d d-m liar. He had not more than got it out of his mouth when he was knocked nearly down. He then ran across the guard line where no one was allowed to follow him. He was only saved by the interference of Colonel Wilson who detailed a guard to conduct him to some place of safety.

While I am writing this letter, I heard that Joseph Elimore was shot by a soldier while shooting at mark with a pistol. The ball entered his head near the temple on the right side, although he is not seriously injured. He belonged to Langston's Company and used to live with one of the Weavers. The ball was nearly spent.

There was a sermon preached on the grounds yesterday by the Rev. Mr. White, the same one that preached in Gettysburg last winter. In the evening, I went to preaching in town at the First Pres. Church.

I expect we will leave this camp next Wednesday. As to where we will go, I can't say for certain although I expect we will go to Camp Dennison.

You will have to excuse the style of this letter as I write sitting on a woodpile with a checkerboard for a writing table.

On October 14, the day the regiment left Camp Clark, the *Springfield Evening News* carried the names of all the personnel of the 44th Regiment together with a brief biography of the officers. Late in the day the men marched through town followed by wagons carrying equipment. The newspaper reported that the procession was "a sight never before equalled in our city." At the Little Miami depot refreshments were served by citizens before the long train of 30 cars pulled out with western Virginia as the regiment's ultimate destination.

The officers and men of the 44th Ohio had anticipated that the regiment would be sent to Kentucky, but instead the regiment moved, via Cincinnati, to the Kanawha Valley in western Virginia.

The citizens of Virginia's 40 counties west of the Allegheny Mountains refused to go along with their Tidewater neighbors to the east and voted overwhelmingly against secession. Steps were commenced which led eventually to the creation of the State of West Virginia. This was a boost to Northern morale and a disappointment to the South. National interest focused on western Virginia during the first year of the war. Here, between May and early July, 1861, the first battles were fought and victories won. Here, the Union's leading general, George B. McClellan, was to gain lightning-like fame.[2]

Notwithstanding the predominant Union sentiment in western Virginia, there was a hard core secessionist minority, and the area suffered much guerrilla warfare during the war as well as forays through the mountains by Confederate forces. It was much easier for the North to occupy and control the area because of its proximity to Ohio. Southern support had to come through the mountains. Occupation of western Virginia was very important to the Union in order to protect the railroad that linked the Ohio Valley with Baltimore, Maryland.

Camp Enyart
Western Virginia
Undated

Piatt's Zouave Regiment is quartered eight or ten miles below us on the river. We are on the same ground that they encamped some time ago. We found one of their sutler's checks which I send you with this letter. Our sutler is with us but has not opened out yet as we only got here yesterday morning. We are all very busy today at fixing our tents and leveling the ground. In reference to the arms that we have got, the flanking companies have the Enfield Rifle and the rest of us have the old muskets rifled out. They are called the Green-

wood Rifles. I expect we will all have the Enfield Rifle before long. I believe that is all I have to say at present only write soon and let me know all the news and if there is anything that you want to know just ask in your letter and I will tell it to you. If we don't make a draw soon, I may not prepay my letters as it is necessary as I am getting short of money in which case you would have to pay it.

To help remedy the shortage of rifles, a contract was awarded by the state of Ohio to Miles Greenwood of Cincinnati to rifle old muskets which had previously been furnished by the federal government to the state. Over 25,000 smoothbore pieces were converted to rifles at a cost of $1.25 a gun. Some of the troops maintained that the "Greenwood rifles" were the equal of the Enfields in range and were superior in destructive power since they carried a heavier shot.[3]

Camp Enyart
October 28, 1861

Having a few leisure moments between drill time, I thought I could not devote it to a better purpose than to let you know how I am getting along.

It is a warm and pleasant day and we have struck our tents and spread our blankets out to dry. We have also just completed a splendid fireplace in our tent. You may think it strange to hear of a fireplace in a tent, but what is it that a Yankee cannot invent when prompted by necessity? It is built in this manner: First, a ditch is dug from the centre of the tent to the outside, about two feet deep and covered with flat stone (which are plenty in this country) sunk six inches below the top of the ground and leaving a mouth of the centre of the tent about one foot square which is the mouth of the fireplace. At the other end, which is outside of the tent there is a chimney about two feet high, so you see we have a complete underground fireplace.

I saw a piece in the Greenville Democrat that stated the troops in this section were poorly clothed and provided for. Of course, we have hardships to undergo that we knew nothing of at home, but I think if Mr. Miller could be here a while to see us, he would make ample acknowledgments for what he has said. We are amply provided with overcoat, blanket, plenty of good wholesome food and, in fact, nearly everything necessary to the comfort of the soldier. Our sutler came a few days ago and by getting an order from the captain we can get anything we want at a reasonable price.

The worst that we are off is for the news as we hardly ever get any news where we are. If there was a battle fought within hearing distance of us, probably you would get the particulars sooner than we would. Day before yesterday, we heard that about 2,000 Sesesh troops were within 15 miles of us and marching on us. We were preparing to meet them when we heard that a brigade had left Gauley to overtake them. I have not heard whether they came in contact or not, but one thing certain they never molested us.

Our company was all out on picket guard last Friday night and part of Saturday (it goes by companies). I had a squad of nine men and was posted about two miles from camp, guarding a road. We had a pretty hard time of it as it was very cold and we were not allowed any fire at night. And to compound it, we all got our feet wet crossing a branch and had to sit out in the open air under a tree.

There is a captain of a Sesesh cavalry company that lives about two miles from camp where he encamped one night last week with 300 cavalry. The next night, they fired into one of our steamers laden with provisions which they were taking to Gauley. There were 32 soldiers in it out of this regiment and four out of our company. They fired several rounds at her and hollered for them to run her ashore and then retreated. They lost ten men and there was only one man hurt in the boat, and he was slightly wounded. You have in this an example of the pluck of the men of which the 44th is composed. I think if they ever attempt to encamp close to our regiment that we will make jailbirds of all of them. We did not know it the other time they camped near us.

The incident on the Kanawha probably took place on October 23, Colonel John N. Clarkson, with a raiding force of Confederates, unsuccessfully attacking the steamer.[4]

I am now writing after night in my tent and in hearing of two prayer meetings which are going on in adjoining tents. They have prayer meeting every night in some of the tents. They take it by turn. There has been a great many converted in the regiment lately. We have preaching every Sunday and a largely attended bible class after sermon. Childs is our regimental chaplain. While I am writing, I hear that two of the hardest cases in the regiment have been converted this evening.

*Camp Enyart
November, 1861*

I would be glad to be at home and see you all if circumstances would permit, but as we are separated far from each other, I expect it will be some time before I will have that privilege. However, I am very well contented with my situation as it is not any harder than I expected to find it.

As I intend to give you a general history of what transpires within the limits of my observation, I will relate a little incident that transpired last week. Last Friday morning, our company was aroused up about 3:00 o'clock in the morning and ordered to provide themselves with arms, ammunition and one day's rations. What to do or where to go, we knew not. Well, by daylight, we were drawn up in line, each man with haversack, blanket, one day's rations, etc. We went down to the landing, embarked on a boat loaded with provisions which we found we were destined to guard to Gauley. It was also rumored that we were to be attacked by 200 Sesesh cavalry. We started about sunup but as the river was very low, our progress was very slow. We had to get out several times to walk several miles on account of the shallowness of the river.

At Clifton, a place about 7 miles up the river, we were detained about four hours while the boat received some repairs and ascended a riffle. It is a small town about the size of New Harrison and is strong secession. The men had either all gone to war or were hid so that we did not get to take any prisoners. However, our first lieutenant and two sergeants had a quite interesting conversation with two young ladies that were strong secessionists. They said they did not hope we would be killed, but they did hope we would be whipped. They made one of the sergeants a present of a secession envelope and a small flag.

While at Clifton, we heard some heavy firing of cannon in the direction of Gauley. When we arrived at Cannelton, a distance of five miles from Gauley, it was nearly dark, and it was unsafe to proceed up the river any farther on account of the Rebel batteries, we hauled up until morning when we unloaded and started for home.

While at Cannelton, we were in sight of where fighting had been done only a few hours before. On our way back, we expected to be attacked every moment, but we were prepared to give them a warm reception. I was placed on the top of the boat behind the breastwork with 15 men under my command; however, we got back without being molested.

Five companies have left our regiment for the fight and consequently the remaining companies have been on almost constant guard duty since they left. We are on regimental guard one day and picket guard the next so that we are pretty well worn out from want of sleep and exposure. I have only got about seven hours sleep out of 48 hours for the last week.

The five companies mentioned by John McKee were ordered to Gauley Bridge and assisted in driving General John B. Floyd from his camp. They were part of General G.W. Benham's Brigade.

Camp Piatt
Western Virginia
November 18, 1861

I was much pleased to find a few lines from Maria in your last letter, and tell her I would like to hear from her every time you write. She wants to know whether I get any chestnuts or not. There are plenty of them in the mountains here but as it is dangerous to go outside of our encampment, I never gathered any although I have bought some from citizens at five cents per pint. There are also plenty of apples here. They sell at 50 cents per bu.

In my last letter, I wrote that some of our regiment had gone out scouting. They started last Monday and returned on Friday with 100 Sesesh cattle, 20 horses, several wagons and 19 prisoners. They made a march of 40 miles. The boys had some hard times as well as good times. They had no tents and sometimes they had to sleep in the open air. One night, it rained on them all night. While they were marching, if they came across a Sesesh house they would take everything that they could make use of that they came across. Their pickets were fired on one night by some 20 rebels but no one was hurt.

The regiment had crossed the Kanawha, marched to Platona, captured the place, and moved on against Colonel A.G. Jenkins at Logan C.H., but the Colonel decamped before their arrival. Chaplain Childs was to write about the raid in a letter (dated November 16th) to the *Springfield Republic,* which published it on November 25th:

"On Monday of the present week, the expedition under Lt. Col. H. Blair Wilson with 400 men, 200 from the 44th Regiment and 200 from the 5th Virginia Regiment, started off over the river for the neighborhood where Col. Jenkins and his rebel cavalry have their headquarters. The expedition was conducted in a most successful manner, showing that Lieut. Col. Wilson, though not a military man, is one of the young destined to make his mark during this campaign. On the second night out their pickets were fired upon. The Col. promptly had his men drawn up in battle array, but the rebels deemed it prudent not to make an attack upon them.

"None of the pickets were injured though the balls whizzed by close to some of them. The Col. and his men returned last night, being out five days, with flying colors with 150 good beeves, and twenty horses, and various other plunder taken from the enemy. So you see the part of the 44th Ohio Regiment remaining here are not idle while the five companies that went up and joined Benham's Brigade a week ago last Sunday are in front rank chasing Floyd pellmell, taking horses, wagons, provisions, etc. The chaplain is thinking about preaching soon from the text, 'What mean the lowing of the cattle and the bleating of the sheep that I hear.' " [5]

> *A sad accident happened here last Friday. As Captain Bell was crossing the river with eleven of his men to go on a picket in a canoe, it was upset and they were all drowned but three privates. In consequence of which, we are ordered by the colonel to appear at dress parade every day for ten days in the position of reversed arms. That makes 10 men we have had drowned in our regiment and not one shot.*
>
> *There is a great deal of speculation in camp in reference to our moving from here. Since Floyd has retreated, I think the fighting is over in this part of Virginia for this winter. Consequently, I think we will go into winter quarters somewhere before long. It may be that we will winter here.*
>
> *Our regiment has the name of being the best regiment along the Kanawha.*

Camp Piatt was located on the Kanawha River at a place, now called Belle, a few miles east of Charleston.[6]

Camp Piatt
Western Virginia
November 24, 1861

I am well and hearty and, as usual, as well as the rest of the boys. Generally, there is very little sickness in camp except colds.

Our arms and accoutrements are generally inspected every Sunday, but we have no inspection today on account of the weather. It commenced snowing about 12:00 o'clock last night and has continued steadily all day. It melts almost as fast as it falls in the valleys, but the hilltops are all covered several inches deep. It is getting colder, and in the morning we may find our streets covered several inches in depth with snow. This is the first snow we have had, but it seems it is commencing in good interest. This is truly bad weather for camping out, but the boys are all in good spirits and manifest a willingness to bear anything for the cause of their country.

There has nothing of importance transpired since I wrote you last except that we are being constantly laid under more restrictions and as I have nothing of much importance to write, I will let you know something of our regulations. In the morning just before daylight, the reveille is beat when we have 15 minutes to get up and fall in for roll call. At daylight, we have drill for one hour, then breakfast, about an hour after which the trumpet sounds and we have two minutes to fall in for drill. At half past ten, the recall is sounded. At 11:00, we have noncommissioned officers' drill for one hour. The noncommissioned officers, viz., corporals and sergeants, are drilled by the major. They are also questioned on Hardee's tactics. In the afternoon, we drill from half past one till half past three, then dress parade from four till five, after which we have supper. At eight o'clock, the tattoo is beat for roll call, 15 minutes after which the taps are beat when every candle is blowed out and everyone is obliged to be in their tents, and no one is allowed to make a noise. From this, you can gather some idea of camp life.

A good joke is in circulation in camp at the expense of Floyd. It is said that in his retreat someone hollered that the

44th regiment was after him, and he understood them to say 44 regiments and commenced marching faster. In their retreat, they burnt almost everything, even down to bowie knives. Several of our boys found bowie knives they had destroyed and thrown away, so you can judge something of the haste with which they retreated.

Camp Piatt
Western Virginia
November 28, 1861

The regiment that was encamped with us leaves this morning. I was detailed yesterday afternoon to take the place of their men on picket and have just been relieved.

When I came to camp I found two of our men ready to go home on sick furloughs, viz: Abe Harman, formerly from Hillgrove and Jacob Brown from near Uncle Alexander's. They have furloughs for sixty days. Jacob Brown said he would be over to see you if he could conveniently.

It snowed all the time last night but this morning it is clear and cold.

Tell the children they must be good children and go to school and learn all they can.

I am glad to hear that Cousin Emma is in Old Darke and I would like very well to see her and welcome her to our northern home during the present national troubles. I hope she will pass the winter among the Belles and Beaux of the Old Buckeye State.

Camp Piatt
Western Virginia
December 2, 1861

I have just come off picket, having been stationed up the river about two miles from camp. I had three men with me, and I told them to stand two hours apiece and relieve each other when I went to a shed and laid down and slept until morning. You can see I had a pretty good time picketing. Our whole company went on picket this morning.

There is about 300 reported sick in the regiment at present although the principal disease is colds caught while on guard. As we have had a great deal of wet weather lately, it is either raining or snowing nearly all the time, I have not been with-

out a cold for almost a month but have always been able to go on duty when called upon.

Captain Langston had a case of desertion in his company last week. It was a person that lived on Michael Beck's farm. They called him Dutch Jake. Please write as soon as you get this letter and let me know whether he is at home or not. Daniel Swarthwood left our company while we were at Camp Clark and we have heard nothing from him since. If he is not at home, let me know it as soon as you can as it may be of considerable importance to me to know where he is if I can find it out soon.

Troops are passing here every few days from Rosecran's army going into winter quarters somewhere in Ohio. Two regiments passed us today. As to where we will quarter, I know nothing about. Some think we will winter in this valley while others think we will go to Camp Dennison.

Matters are getting rather dull here as the Sesesh have all left this part of the country, and we have nothing to liven up the times. If it is not too much trouble, I would like if you would send me a paper occasionally as I hardly ever get any news here. We get to know very little of what is going on outside of our camp.

Although in his letters John McKee attempted to downplay the hardships caused by adverse weather conditions in order not to cause too much concern at home, it is quite evident that the winter was causing much to be concerned about. In the *Springfield Republic* the following item appeared on Friday, December 6, 1861:

"We are advised accurately as to the sanitary condition of the 44th Regiment, up to Thursday last — Thanksgiving. The highest number at any time reported unfit for duty was ninety, on Friday last, but of these only thirty were in hospital, the others only slightly ailing and were attended at their tents.

"The prevailing complaints were such as result from cold and wet exposures, coughs, diarrhea, dysentery and some rheumatism, with only two cases of fever, which at the date named had yielded to treatment. The situation of the regiment is anything but pleasant, in consequence of the almost incessant rain and cold. The camp is a mud puddle, and a change in the quarters must be made, or a fearful amount of disease, and perhaps many deaths, must ensue. The officers were earnestly appealing for a removal to Kentucky, and in the hope of success. Before this time, if not ordered to Kentucky, the erection of winter quarters will doubtless be begun by the 44th." [7]

Moreover, Colonel Gilbert personally wrote to departmental headquarters complaining about the lack of proper care for his regiment. Written on December 3, 1861, at Camp Piatt, this unusual letter, in parte, is as follows:

"At the risk of being considered impertinent I will again call the attention of the Commanding General to the rapid depreciation of the materiel of my regiment the most of which is attributable to insufficient shelter and clothing. It is now more than three weeks since my requisitions were sent in and no lumber or coats or shoes or flannel shirts or socks have been received! If it is the intention to keep us here I shall be glad to receive some notice to that effect and some materiel to make my men more comfortable. It is hard for me to see them broken down by exposure that could be so easily avoided, and discouraging to know when service may be demanded of us we will probably not be in condition to render it.

"I do not mean to be, or even to feel, insubordinate but if we do not get some attention such feelings will arise! This regiment was raised under promises to the officers and men, myself excepted, that they should serve in Missouri or Kentucky. They came here in answer to a supposed emergency which no longer exists. And, as the certainty of being kept here seems to be closing in upon their minds, I have trouble enough to reconcile them to the disappointment, without the additional drawback of what appears to be unnecessary hardship in the way of deficient shelter and clothing.

"I have given the Surgeon an order to go to Springfield, Ohio, where the regiment was raised to get donations for our sick; they at least must be cared for."

On December 8, 1861, Col. Gilbert ordered the regimental surgeon, Major Henry K. Stute, to return to Springfield for twenty days to make representation to the friends of the regiment to secure donations of comforts and to have requisitions for hospital store filled.[8]

Camp Piatt
Western Virginia
December 12, 1861
Maria wants to know if we have preaching in our camp. We have preaching every Sabbath afternoon when the state of the weather will permit us to have it out of doors as we have no church to have it in as you have in Darke County. We have

to go under review and inspection of arms on Sunday which occupies the forenoon.

Willie wonders how we get along this cold weather. I suppose it is not as cold here as it is in Darke County. For the last week, it has been very warm for this time of the year. We can drill very comfortably today in our shirt sleeves. Although it has snowed some this winter here, we have had very little freezing weather. Willie said you have killed five rabbits this winter. If he were here he could find larger game than rabbits. I saw a man yesterday who said he had killed five bear and several deer this fall. I also heard of a boy that killed two bear and one wildcat.

You wrote that you had heard the mud was knee deep in camp. I supposed you were well enough posted not to credit stories of that kind when you hear them from such persons as Charles Flemming. I can walk all over the campground without getting my boots muddy, although several weeks ago we had a great deal of rain and consequently it was pretty muddy for a while.

As to those men that were drowned, they started in behind the boat after which the boat which was going downstream turned around to come up to the landing, when owing to a want of skill in rowing the skiff it floated against the boat. They might have all been saved yet had they not tried to climb on the boat (which several succeeded in doing) and by this means upsetting the skiff. The captain saw this and commanded them to sit still, but they were scared so they did not mind him.

One of our regiment died in the hospital this week with some kind of fever, it being the first death from sickness we have had. He was a private in Captain Shaffer's company and was buried with the honors of war.

Our company is building winter quarters at present. The government would not furnish us with boards so we are building them with logs which we cut and slid down the mountain. We can cut them at the top of the mountain and slide them within 100 yards of where we are building. When we start them at the top, they go down with a perfect rush making everything jingle.

The New Harrison boys talk of sending home for a box of things, and, if they do, I may get you to send some things along. I don't need any clothes, but I would like to have some butter, sausage and honey or almost anything good to eat. We have plenty of meat but it is fat pork and something that resembles beef in color but India rubber in toughness. I have lived mostly on pilot bread for some time. We can get butter at the sutler's at 25 cents per pound, but that is rather steep living. It is a very inferior article at that. I would almost give one dollar for a good meal but still we fare as well as I expected to and am therefore very well contented.

Camp Piatt
Western Virginia
December 18, 1861

For the last week, we have had very nice warm weather which has considerably improved the health in the regiment so that things are beginning to wear a little more favorable aspect.

It is settled now that we are to stay here this winter, and we are making active preparations for wintering. We have received 100,000 rations and lumber enough to build shanties for the whole regiment, besides a hospital which they are now building and is to be 80 feet long and a horse stable large enough to hold 300 horses, so that in a short time we will be well fixed for spending the winter.

Our regiment has lately been increased by the addition of a cavalry company. We also have one piece of artillery belonging to us.

William Hayes says he sent home for some things. I did not know it until he had sent the letter off. I would like if you would join with him and send me something good to eat. All it will cost you will be the freight to Cincinnati. Also please send my silver pen holder as it will be handy to carry.

The paymaster called around to pay us off the other day, but the muster rolls were not made out right and consequently we will not be paid off until next month when I suppose we will be paid for four months service.

One of Langston's sergeants has been under arrest for three or four days for letting a man go on guard mounting with a hat on instead of a military cap.

While I am writing this, they have detailed a sergeant and two men to go on a scout of some kind. I have heard it *reported that Ohio would not receive any more volunteers. Please write whether it is so or not.*

*Camp Piatt
Western Virginia
Christmas — December 25, 1861*

The weather still remains warm with the exception of an occasional blustery day. We have received boards and are busy building winter houses. We build them long enough for a whole company and then put partitions in making five rooms. We will have stoves in them which will make them pretty comfortable.

I think the company you spoke of would be very desirable company as most of your officers I think are well versed in — I was going to say military, but I believe I will say culinary affairs. My idea of northern chivalry has considerably expanded since I heard that the young ladies were getting up companies.

I was very agreeably surprised last Saturday to see Scipio Meyers and Levi Gilbert in our camp. They had been at Washington and were on their way home. Levi left for home the next day but Meyers still remains with us.

We traded coffee for about twenty chickens today and had a big Christmas dinner. A good many of the boys went to Malden today to have a Christmas spree. You wrote that you wanted me to come home during the holidays, but there is no chance to get a furlough for a while yet but I will come home as soon as I can get a furlough.

1862

1862

Camp Piatt
Western Virginia
January 1, 1862

We have done no drilling for some time in order to finish our quarters which are nearly completed. They are built in the form of a hollow square and when we get them finished I think they will make neat as well as comfortable winter quarters.

The weather still remains pleasant and the health of the regiment is still improving. There was only two reported sick in our company this morning and they only complained of slight colds.

We will get dress suits in a few days. They are in camp and some of them have been issued out. We will get dark blue frock coats and sky blue pants. The colonel has not decided yet whether to get hats or caps.

We have taken a good many Sesesh prisoners lately among which was a Sesesh captain which our cavalry took a few days ago. He was tried and sent to Boston Harbor as prisoner of war.

I am writing this on New Year's Day but I am not spending the day quite as pleasantly as though I was at home to spend it with you. It almost seems to me I can see you and Maria and Willie and Irvie and Emma at school having an exhibition or a treat from your teacher or if neither enjoying yourselves in some pleasant manner.

Camp Piatt
Western Virginia
January 23, 1862

I am still enjoying very good health. I believe I have never had better health than I have had since I enlisted.

Mother says you are going to have a protracted meeting in three weeks and wants to know if I can be with them at that time. I don't know whether I can get a furlough at that time or not. The colonel is not giving many furloughs at this time and then only in urgent cases.

Since I wrote to you last we have received our dress suits which I believe I have described to you in a previous letter. We have also received Enfield rifles instead of our old corn stalk muskets as the boys call them. Since we have finished our quarters we have to commence our lessons again in Hardee. The sergeants and two corporals selected by the captain recite to the colonel. The balance of the corporals and four privates selected by the captain from among the privates recite to captains of some company besides their own. I was one that was selected by the captain to recite to the colonel. We have to get lessons of about fifteen pages each and recite every other evening.

Aaron Derchen paid us a visit of a few days and returned this morning. The boys were all very glad to see someone from America as they expressed it.

If you would send me some postage stamps the next time you write it would be doing me a great favor as we cannot get them here and they come very good when I write to some persons that I would not like to have pay the postage. I think we will get paid off soon when I will have some money to send home and enough left to buy these things.

Camp Piatt
Western Virginia
February 11, 1862

I have just heard that Abe Shields has obtained a furlough and will start for home tomorrow morning and I sit down in haste to write you a few lines to send with him. I saw Tom Orr a few days ago and he said he had seen Father and had heard from him that you were going to send a box with Abe Zimmerman for me and as his time was nearly due I delayed writing until he arrived but I understand he took sick and has not arrived yet. I am still enjoying good health and am in good spirits.

In order to give you some idea of how we are spending our time now, I will give you a programme of our drill hours.

From 9 a.m. to 10 a.m. we drill the Chassens drill (or in other words without arms) in which all the evolutions are performed in double quick time. From 10:15 a.m. to 12 a.m. in light infantry drill with arms. From 1:30 p.m. to 4 p.m. battalion drill. At 4:30 p.m. dress parade when we have to come out in our dress suits and with shoes blacked. Every other day in the forenoon, instead of drilling as before stated, we drill three hours in the skirmish drill and as that takes a good deal of room we march at double quick about two miles from camp to a large meadow.

The noncommissioned officers' recitations are still kept up. We recite twice a week to the colonel. We have went through the first volume Hardee and are now reviewing.

This programme may be tedious to you but I write it in order to give you some idea of camp life.

The colonel has been very strict with noncommissioned officers. This winter he has reduced to ranks four corporals and one sergeant in our company. One of our corporals was reduced this week for passing a counterfeit half dollar to a citizen who brought pies in camp to sell.

By special Order No. 5 Corporal William B. Galloway was reduced to ranks "for violation of the 33rd Article of War. He having passed a counterfeit piece of money to a person selling provisions in camp." [1] The order was signed by Lt. Col. A.B. Wilson. About two weeks later the pie trade was prohibited "for the promotion of health in the camp." Corporal Galloway transferred with the regiment when it reorganized as the 8th Ohio Volunteer Cavalry, became commissary sergeant for the company and was killed on October 29, 1864, in the battle of Beverly, West Virginia.[2]

We still have the luck to get hold of a Sesesh occasionally. There were several brought in today, one of which said he had just deserted from Floyd's Army and came to give himself up.

I heard that Cousin Emma had received a letter from her father. Let me know whether it is so or not. I should hardly think she could get a letter from Carolina.

If you have not sent me any postage stamps yet you will please send me some when you answer this.

Charles Maus arrived in camp on last Monday. The boys were all glad to see him.

Camp Piatt
Western Virginia
February 16, 1862

I just came off picket this morning where I had a pretty cool night of it. The weather has been pretty cool for the last few days. It was snowing when I went out but after it had snowed about two inches deep it quit snowing and got cold. However, it is thawing pretty fast today.

In reference to me going home on furlough I suppose I will have to give it up for the present as the colonel has decided not to let any of the noncommissioned officers go home at present as he wishes them to spend the time in studying Hardee. As to when I can obtain a furlough I cannot say. They only allow three privates to go home at a time and those get to go home first who can present the most plausible excuse.

Our regiment was paid off yesterday but we were not paid off for near all the time we have been out. I received about thirty dollars.

Camp Piatt
Western Virginia
February 23, 1862

The weather still remains warm, and we have had a great deal of rain which has considerably raised the river. But we are not put to much inconvenience on account of the mud as we have our streets paved with coal cinders which we obtained at the salt works. We had 10 four-horse teams hauling cinders for 20 days to put on the parade grounds and sidewalks.

A rather amusing incident occurred in camp one day last week. It was as follows: A deck hand on a boat, that had been laying at the wharf for some time, was in the habit of selling whiskey to the soldiers which is against the orders of the colonel, for which he was brought to the centre of the parade grounds and here his head was shaved after which he was placed in front of seven men at charge bayonets and in this position he was drummed out of camp by all the drums in the regiment playing the Rogues' March. Although it was snowing at the time, he was made to march out in his shirt sleeves and bare head.

Yesterday being the anniversary of Washington's birthday was kept by our regiment as a holiday. In the afternoon the regiment was called out and the lieutenant colonel read Washington's farewell address, after which our little barker in the shape of a twelve-pounder was brought out and five shells were fired at an old house about one mile off and it was struck once, the other shells falling near the house bursting the moment they struck ground.

Enclosed you will find twenty dollars which you will give to father to keep for me. In case we should not be paid off for a good while or if anything should happen, I may call on him for part of it. We do not get near all our wages as a great part of it goes for clothing. We have more clothes than we need, but they are forced on us. The men have all drawn about twenty dollars worth of clothing more than they are allowed up to this time which will be deducted from their wages.

Our cavalry captured a Sesesh colonel last week by the name of Miller. He was home on furlough when they got wind of him and they took him unawares. He was one of the Sesesh leaders in this part of the country and was instrumental in drafting a great many Union men.

Camp Piatt
Western Virginia
March 19, 1862

The box of provisions of which you spoke has not arrived yet. I suppose they are detained in Cincinnati as there are not many boats running from there to this point at this time. They are using all the boats they can raise to carry transportation to the Mississippi. I suppose they will arrive in a few days.

We are having our camp decorated with cedar trees which gives it a very nice appearance. We can get plenty of them within two hundred yards of our camp.

All the objection I have to our parade ground is that it does not get muddy enough and consequently we have too much drilling to do.

We are occasionally successful in catching some of the rebel bushwackers. One day this week our cavalry brought in a Sesesh lieutenant, orderly sergeant, and a private.

The weather is getting tolerably warm in this part of the country. The trees are beginning to leaf and the plum blossoms are out in full bloom. The farmers will plant corn here about the first of April.

The bon ton ladies of this country are all Sesesh. One day last week several of them were looking at some envelopes when one of them says, "Oh! Look! Here is one with the American flag on it. What a detestable thing it is. Give me one with the <u>staas</u> and <u>baas</u> on it." This is the specimen of the Virginia F.F.V.s.

There is bear meat offered for sale in camp every day or two. It is sold for 15 cents per lb. That species of game is tolerably abundant in this country.

*Camp Piatt
Western Virginia
March 23, 1862*

The box was detained for sometime in Cincinnati waiting for a boat and was about two weeks on the way. Consequently, some of the things were a little spoiled but my box kept better than any of the rest of the things that were started at the time it was sent. I am much obliged to you for all the good things you sent. It was hardly necessary for you to write how to cook those white puddings which you sent me as I had one of them cooked and eaten before I received the letter. They are the best things I have tasted since I left home and the boys all say they are the best puddings they ever tasted. I think mother never misses it in making a white pudding. I think sheet iron crackers will have to give way to sweet and light cakes for a while.

Father wrote in his letter that he heard we were removed to Winchester, Virginia. I think when he gets as used to reports of that kind as I am he will not pay much attention to them. When we leave here, if we leave at all before we are discharged, neither the papers or any of us but our field officers will in all probability know anything of it more than ten or twelve hours before we leave. The most creditable report I have heard is that we are going to Bull Island on Lake Erie and ten miles from upper Sandusky to guard prisoners. The major, it is said, gave it as his opinion that would be our destination. This does not at all suit the boys as they would rather go where there is fighting to do. We got marching orders one evening about two months ago, but it was countermanded at four o'clock in the morning.

We are now drilling with our knapsack, haversack, can-

teen, overcoat and blanket in addition to our arms and accoutrements which makes it very tiresome drilling. It is done in order to make us hardy.

We will be reviewed and inspected today by General Cox and have made great arrangements for the occasion. We have decorated the grounds with cedar trees which are plenty within a half mile of camp.

Camp Piatt
Western Virginia
April 2, 1862

The spring which in this part of the country has been very wet and backward has at last come out warm and beautiful. The frequent and heavy showers of rain have given way to timely and warm growing showers. Old dame nature seems to be revived and is ruling things with a milder hand.

Last Sunday, Sergeants Tate, Creeger and myself procured a pass and started out of camp with the purpose of taking a walk through the country. After walking about two miles and feeling warm and fatigued we went into a house to rest ourselves and have a chat with some of our neighbors and as they proved to be Sesesh neighbors.

The husband and one brother are in the Sesesh Army and consequently we found only the old lady with several rather good looking daughters and one son about seventeen years of age besides several smaller children among which was one just beginning to crawl which they called Jeffey.

Jeffey was a little troublesome and of course his name had to be called every few minutes while we were there. Eventually someone passed a remark about a nice brood of chickens which were running around in the yard. Someone said she would have a good chance to sell them if our regiment stayed here this summer. "Oh," said she, "if I were to raise two hundred I would not sell one to the **Union** army." Had a man talked to us in that manner we would have taken him along to camp but a woman's tongue is generally at liberty to wag at its own discretion.

Since the weather has become warmer the boys have been putting in their spare time at catching fish of which the Kanawha furnishes a great abundance and of choice varieties. The most common kinds are bass, sturgeon and a species of catfish similar but different in some respects to our Darke County catfish. We frequently catch them two feet long. The sturgeon is the most beautiful fish I ever saw. It resembles a juke in shape but has large and hard scales. They are generally about 18 inches long.

I would like to be at home helping you to make molasses. I am sorry I did not get the wax mother was so kind as to make for me. Tell her I am much obliged to her for her trouble although I did not get the wax. I suppose the children enjoy themselves fine helping to make molasses especially about time to stir off.

The paymaster paid us a visit last week and paid us for two months which is twenty-six dollars but the boys were not much the better off for it as their clothing and sutler's bill in most cases amounted to more than their wages. My clothing bill was fifteen dollars. There will be nothing more deducted out for clothing after this until the end of six months nor will the clothing bill be as heavy for the next six months as it was for the first six as we now have nearly enough clothes to do us for the next six months. My clothing bill up to this time is $36.00 and my allowance is $21.00 which leaves $15.00 which was deducted out of my wages.

Camp Piatt
Western Virginia
April 20, 1862

William Hayes has not been able to drill for some time on account of something like the rheumatism in the leg. He has got the position of tending to the field officers' horses, seven in number. It will be easy work for him as all he will have to do will be to attend to the horses.

I received a letter today from Wm. A. Horner. He is at Winchester, Virginia, and was in the fight they had at that place. He said when they were following Jackson they were five days without rations, forage or even blankets. They had to subsist on anything they could find along the road.

Our pickets were fired into one night this week by some Sesesh bushwhacker. We sent a patrol out after him but did not succeed in overhauling him.

The colonel has issued an order that anyone found six feet from his gun shall be court-martialed.

We sent two companies of infantry and one of cavalry on a scout yesterday. They took rations for ten days.

On May 1, 1862, the 44th moved upstream from Camp Piatt, which was on the Kanawha River near Charleston, to a place near the junction of the Gauley and New Rivers which unite to form the Kanawha. Here they were to guard a bridge over the Gauley which had been rebuilt after its destruction by Confederate General Henry A. Wise when his army had retreated the previous summer.

At Gauley Bridge the regiment was brigaded with the 36th and 47th Ohio under Colonel George Crook who was destined to become a major general before the war was over and after the war a successful Indian fighter in the West.

Camp Gauley
Western Virginia
May 3, 1862

Last Saturday evening at dress parade our regiment was ordered to be ready to march by the next Tuesday morning at daylight which of course was the best news we have heard for some time. The boys could hardly wait until the time came to start.

When Tuesday morning came, notwithstanding it was raining steadily all the time, we were called up in line of battle at 7 a.m. and about 9 a.m. we started. As the roads were very bad (being about shoemouth deep) our progress was very slow as the teams would frequently stall which would stop the whole train.

Although we did not travel very fast, it was the hardest day's work I ever done. The first day's traveling is always the hardest for a soldier. We marched 13 miles the first day. Counting our knapsack, gun and accoutrements, etc., we had a load of over 40 lbs. apiece to carry, which is no small load to carry all day.

On April 29th, each enlisted man was ordered to carry "his arms, and accoutrements with 40 rounds of ammunition, knapsack with two shirts, two pair drawers, three pair socks, one pair pants, one woolen blanket, one overcoat, one tin cup, one tin plate, one knife, fork and spoon, one haversack, one canteen." [3]

The second day we only traveled a distance of five miles

Camp near Gauley Bridge, Western Virginia, 1862

as our progress was impeded very much by landslides, but I suppose you do not know what they are. Well, I will tell you.

The road runs on the bank of the river and was cut along the side of hills which were mostly from a quarter to a half mile high and in some places nearly perpendicular, and in wet weather the ground will start at the top and gather force until it becomes an avalanche of mud and covers the road to the depth of several feet. We detailed a corps of eighty men to act as pioneers to bridge these places. They had to cut brush, throw them on and shovel dirt on top of it so that the wagons could drive over. Infantry could go around these places but we had to keep in sight of the wagons.

Today, having good roads, we traveled at the rate of about twenty-three miles per day and are now stationed at Gauley where I suppose we will stay until we are brigaded, which will be in a week or two.

Camp Gauley Bridge
Western Virginia
May 1862

Now I will give you some idea of our present encampment. The Kanawha River, as I suppose you are aware, is formed by the uniting of Gauley and New Rivers. The town of Gauley is situated on the east side of this junction. It is a town of no importance except in a military point of view, not being any larger than Hillgrove.

Gauley Bridge of which you have heard so much is across Gauley River and near its mouth. It was burnt by Wise in his retreat but has since been rebuilt by the government. It is a wire suspension bridge. I was on guard at the bridge last Tuesday.

When we came here we found one battery of artillery, two companies of cavalry and two regiments of infantry. They have all left since but the cavalry. I wrote to you that there was a probability of us leaving here soon but the general impression is now that we will remain here for some time.

The 47th Ohio is encamped 3 miles from here on a large hill. We can see them drilling plainly. Cotton Hill, of which you have probably heard is in sight of this place. It is about 3 miles off. Our camp is situated on a hill from which we have a fine view of the surrounding country for several miles but it is so hilly that I can see but one farm and that is occupied by the 47th as a camping ground. The rest is all a wilderness of hills.

Tell mother she need not be uneasy about me eating at Sesesh houses as our colonel does not give us a chance to do so. Since we came here it is a very punishable offense to go into a neighbor's house.

Camp Gauley Bridge
Western Virginia
May 1862

As we have marching orders and will leave today some time, I thought I would write a line to you and let you know it. I do not know where we are going to but I suppose it will be in the direction of Lewisburg.

Camp Lewisburg
Western Virginia
May 15, 1862

After two days and a half of hard marching we are encamped in the town of Lewisburg. If you look at the map, you will find that it lays sixteen miles from the Allegheny Mountains. It is a town some larger than Greenville and is the nicest town for the size I have seen in this state. It has been in the hands of the Confederates until last Monday morning when a detachment of the 44th numbering about 760 and about one hundred of the 48th Ohio, after a slight skirmish, drove the enemy (numbering about 200) out and took possession of the town.

The enemy only fired a couple of rounds and skedaddled leaving everything behind them; a great many even leaving their guns in their haste to light out. We wounded one and captured five of their cavalry. The one that was wounded is in our hands and it is thought his wounds will prove fatal. Our men pursued them to within two miles of the White Sulphur Springs which is eight miles from here.

To give you some idea of a forced march I will tell you a few things about our march here. We started from Gauley at 5 p.m. Sunday and marched til eleven that night. Started the next morning at daylight and marched until 12 at night. Rested til 3 and marched five miles before breakfast. The next *night we marched until 12 o'clock and started the next morning at daylight. Reached Lewisburg at 10 a.m., a distance of 62 miles. The road was so hilly that we were either going up or down hill all the time. The second night we encamped on the top of Sewell Mountain.*

The rebels have spent a great deal of labor in building fortifications between here and Gauley but they deserted them when they heard of our advance.

To give you some idea of the state to which this country is reduced, I will give you the price of a few leading articles: Coffee $1.25 per lb.; sugar $.75 per lb.; flour $5.00 per hundred; shoes $5.00; boots $15.00; suede boots $18.00 and other things in proportion. Although these figures look large, I know them to be facts.

The brigade moved to Lewisburg and from there the 44th crossed into the mountains, penetrating Confederate territory as far as 10 miles beyond Covington at Jackson River Depot on the Virginia Central Railroad. During this raid, railroad tracks and a bridge were destroyed before withdrawing to Lewisburg.

On the night of May 22nd, a Confederate force of 2,500 men, under command of General Henry H. Heth, reached the vicinity of Lewisburg and at about five o'clock in the morning of the 23rd opened fire on the Federal troops, numbering about 1,200 men. It was the 44th Ohio's (and John McKee's) first real battle.

Camp Lewisburg
Western Virginia
May 24, 1862

I have been on a scout across the Alleghenies passing through the White Sulphur Springs which is at the foot of the mountains and Covington which is across the mountains and on to Jackson Station on the railroad which is forty miles from here. We made the trip without seeing any Sesesh troops except a few who were home on furlough. We took ten prisoners in all.

Yesterday morning at daybreak, we were attacked by over three thousand rebels under General Heth. Although there were only about fifteen hundred of us, we succeeded in com-

The Lewisburg Cannon

One of the four guns captured in the action at Lewisburg was believed to have been originally used by the British in the Revolutionary War and captured at Yorktown when Lord Cornwallis surrendered. The gun was kept as a museum piece at the Norfolk Navy Yard until the Civil War when it was pressed into service on behalf of the Confederacy. Following its capture at Lewisburg, permission was granted to take the gun to Springfield, Ohio, where it is presently mounted in front of Memorial Hall. [5]

pletely routing them after fighting about an hour and a half. They made their appearance about daylight when our regiment was immediately called into line of battle when they immediately commenced shelling us from an opposite hill.

Companies B and D were sent to engage them in the front. The 36th and our regiment were sent to attack the flanks. At the command "forward" we all started off on quick time and in the short space of 20 minutes we had in our possession four out of six of their field pieces and the other two were in full retreat thus silencing their whole battery.

When the rebels found that we had silenced all their pieces, they commenced to waver and soon they were in full retreat in such haste that the road over which they went was literally strewn with blankets, overcoats, pistols, knives, guns, cartridge boxes, etc. A great many in their haste did not take time to take their accoutrements off but just took out their knives and cut the straps in two letting them drop in the road. Our wagons have gathered up about 500 stand of arms while wagon after wagon might be filled with clothes that are laying along the road.

The casualties in our regiment is 6 killed and 14 wounded, among which are John Reck, son of Samuel Reck, and Alspaugh, a little fellow that used to live at Trumps and worked at the carpenter trade. Captain Langston was slightly wounded in the foot. Although our company was in the thickest of the fight, it came off without anyone being hurt. Part of the time we were crouched down under a fence while the shots passed over us like hail. One shell bursted nearly over our company but did no damage and a ball passed just over our heads.

The loss of the 36th is about the same as our regiment while the rebels left about 60 of their dead on the field and about the same number wounded with 150 prisoners.

I do not know whether I hit anyone or not but I had several fair shots at the distance of about one hundred yards and do not think I was any more excited than if I were shooting at a squirrel.

On May 23, Colonel Gilbert issued the following order of congratulations: "Soldiers of the 44th Regiment. I congratulate you upon the soldier-like manner in which you have this day performed your duty. It is the reward of the labor you have been at in attaining that good state of discipline which alone can secure that morale which renders you irresistible.

"I am assured by your conduct this day that whilst our country has such men for its defenders, our mothers, wives and children need not fear its destruction at the hands of the base scoundrels who are in arms against us.

"Soldiers, I am proud of your success and ask no higher glory than to lead you on to new actions." [4]

Meadow Bluffs
Western Virginia
June 13, 1862

Our surgeons accompanied by a squad of cavalry were going to Lewisburg yesterday to attend to some wounded rebels that were left there. They met about 500 cavalry with two companies of infantry. They immediately sent word to camp when our regiment was ordered to be ready to march in one hour. We started after them thinking it was the advanced guard of a large army and intending to hold them in check until the rest of the force would be ready to resist an attack or retreat in case the force proved too large for us.

We marched about 7 miles when we found it was only a foraging party sent to a mill to get flour. We bivouacked there for the night and returned to camp this morning.

Camp Meadow Bluffs
Western Virginia
June 17, 1862

We have three regiments infantry, viz., 44th, 36th, 47th, Ohio; 500 cavalry, four mountain howitzers (or jackass batteries) and two ten-pounder rifled Parrott guns. Father, you say, thinks we are not strong enough to hold our position where we are. I suppose we are not as near the railroad as he thinks we are. We are a distance of 50 miles from the nearest point on the railroad. Lewisburg may still be said to be in our possession as we only fell back here to gain a better position and make our supplies nearer.

Our scouts are in Lewisburg every day or two. The nearest rebel encampment is at Union, 35 miles beyond Lewisburg. Skirmishes frequently take place between our scouts (principally cavalry) and those of the rebels. They had one last week in which our cavalry succeeded in killing five or six among which was a lieutenant.

Since the battle at Lewisburg, a great many of Heth's army have deserted and come here to give themselves up. The greater part of them were let go on parole. One squad of eight came in yesterday and another of eleven came today.

You ask if any member of Co. B or G run in time of battle. I am satisfied that no one of those companies run and I think I am safe in saying there was not a man in the regiment that shrunk from his duty. I know that some of the boys were so anxious to go ahead that Captain Newkirk had to keep saying "steady, boys, not so fast — back to your places, not so fast, you will be shot by your own men." C. Anderson got so far ahead of his company as to be right between the two fires. Our company was so situated that by going too fast it would interfere with other companies or doubtless our captain would have let us pitch in to suit ourselves.

Since the battle, I have often wondered how men could go into a battle under as little excitement as we went into that one. They commenced throwing bombs at us while we were eating and I set my tin of coffee in my bunk, got my gun and then tied my shoestrings tighter, took a look at my cartridges to see they were all right and was then ready to start. Although part of the time we were in the woods, I saw very few take shelter behind trees but most of them pushed on to get near to the rebels.

A little circumstance happened in the thickest of the fight which caused a great deal of laughter. One of the enemy wishing to desert the rebel army slipped away from his company and came running toward us with a white pocket handkerchief on the end of his gun hollering, "Don't shoot me, I was forced into it." We sent him to the rear as a prisoner.

Camp Meadow Bluffs
Western Virginia
July 6, 1862

We have been on a scout something similar to the Jackson River dash. One week ago last Friday we were ordered to be ready by the next morning at daylight to march in light marching orders, i.e.; rubber and woolen blankets, canteen, haversack with two days' provisions, gun and accoutrements.

We also had two days' rations in the wagons.

The next morning we were ready at the appointed time but the order to march did not come. We laid around all day expecting to leave at any moment and at night received the same orders for the next day but this time we were not doomed to disappointment, but started for Union which is forty miles from here and near the foot of the Allegheny Mountains.

The first day we marched, we did not see any signs of rebels but the next day when within 15 miles of Union we run across 40 cavalry which they had sent out to ascertain our numbers and the road we would take. The first we knew of their approach was the word came back, "cavalry coming like hell!" and the next was "Macy is taken prisoner." When the two who were in front saw them coming they made for the advanced guard after firing their guns but the cavalry came upon them so fast that they were overtaken. When one of the cavalry who had a faster horse than the balance came up to the guard who was in advance. He ordered him to surrender and give up his gun, at the same time drawing his sabre over his head. The guard turned around and while pretending to hand his gun up, shot the rebel's horse, and before the cavalryman got disentangled from his horse the guard was hid in the woods. They made the other guard give up his gun, accoutrements, blanket, haversack, etc., and was starting off when our cavalry came in sight. They then fled, leaving their prisoner.

Our cavalry pursued them and succeeded in killing one of their horses and taking its rider prisoner. They also captured the other cavalryman whose horse was shot.

That night we encamped within two miles of their camp intending to make a breakfast job of them. But the next day when we went into their camp, although they had the advantage in numbers and choice of position, they had fled. We had to be contented with taking several barrels of crackers and sugar, 15 or 20 horses and 300 cattle which they had left behind. We then started for Meadow Bluffs where we arrived at noon of the fourth day, making the distance of over 80 miles in 3-1/2 days. The last half day we marched 17 miles, which showed we were good for a few miles more if necessary. I think the 44th can travel or fight with anything that is out.

I believe you asked a few questions that I forgot to answer — we can get plenty of butter here at 25¢ per lb., eggs sell at 25¢ per dozen. As to sending butter and eggs here, I would have no possible way of getting them from Gauley here. You also wanted to know if we get any knicknacks here. Our sutler brings on cakes and candy to sell but as every wagonload costs about $50 to get it hauled, of course he sells very dear. As the citizens can hardly get flour at $15 per barrel, they charge almost as high as the sutler. Some of the boys have paid as high as one dollar for a loaf of bread.

When it comes to fruit, it is very plentiful. We can buy strawberries for 6¢ a quart and cherries for 25¢ per gallon or by getting a pass we can get them for the picking. I was out on a pass yesterday and on one farm, I found cherries enough, blackheart cherries, to supply a town as large as Gettysburg. The hills around here are full of huckleberries which will be ripe in a few weeks and there will be an abundance of peaches in their turn.

Enclosed you will find a song which was composed by a private in Co. C of this regiment.

They are not cutting wheat here yet but I understand that in the Kanahwa Valley they are through with harvest. It is a great deal cooler here among the mountains than it is in places that are north of here. I have seen very little corn here that is knee high yet. Wheat is good.

P.S. The soldier that proved himself so brave in shooting the rebel's horse, after being commanded to surrender, is now in the guardhouse for taking something from Sesesh on the scout. I think that is very poor reward for his bravery.

Meadow Bluffs
Western Virginia
July 13, 1862

It is rather amusing to hear the reports that have reached Darke County in reference to our fight in Lewisburg. In the first place, Daniel Garret at the time of the fight, was a bugler (he is now a fifer) and I suppose he would not be likely to do much fighting with a bugle. If he was in the fight at all, his place was near the commander of the company in order to sound the signals. And, secondly, Company B was on the extreme left of the battalion and did not come in contact with the cannon only at long musket range, probably two hundred yards. The cannon were all opposite the center of the battalion. I do not by any means pretend to say that Company B did no good fighting but to the contrary they stood up bravely against a very heavy fire of musketry.

The rebels did have one of their cannon loaded with grapeshot and aimed at the right of the battalion and were just in the act of firing it when he was shot by Captain Stough of Company F which was near the center of the battalion.

I think Calvin Hays is considerably mistaken about having to eat horse meat while a prisoner. His father says he thinks it is a story of Cal's own make. He may have had to eat some rather tough meat but I think there was no horse about it. I have seen a good many persons that have been prisoners and a good many rebel soldiers and, from what I can learn from them, I think a great many of these big stories are fictitious, told by someone desirous of making himself a great hero. The prisoners that we take are just as well taken care of as our own soldiers are. A scouting party from our regiment took a rebel soldier who was home on a furlough last week, and his mother said she was glad he was taken, as he was in no danger now of being killed while he was in our hands. He is only about 18 years old and seems to be quite intelligent.

Maria wants to know how I like our present place of encampment. We are all very well satisfied. We are encamped on a large hill which is one of a range called the Meadow Bluffs. We are in a nice grove of chestnut and oak trees, and as it is an elevated position there is always an air stirring which makes it very cool and pleasant. By going about a half mile from our camp we can have a very fine view of the surrounding country and of the Allegheny Mountains which are over twenty miles off.

She also wants to know if I have seen any very big mountains. Since I have been in Virginia, I have seen nothing else but mountains and hills. Some of the mountains, such as Sewel, Meadow and the Alleghenies, are tolerable large. It costs as much to build some of the roads in this country as it does to build a railroad in Ohio. They are cut on the sides of hills in many places that are as steep as a house roof. On the side of the road there will be a cut probably 10 feet deep, while on the other side one can look apparently almost straight down.

In many places, they are cut in this way through solid rock.

There are a great many huckleberries in the vicinity of our camp. They are about the size of small currants at this time.

While out last week, a scouting party from our regiment came across 80 cavalry that were encamping about 20 miles from here and were laying in ambush to entrap them when a cavalry company from Cox's brigade came up and thinking they were rebels , fired some 200 shots at them. Before they found out their mistake, our scouts were between the rebel pickets and their camp and the cavalry after running their pickets in of course did not expect to find a friend in that position. The cavalry then started after the rebels but they had too much the start and got away. We got two of their pickets and killed one. No one was hurt on our side.

Meadow Bluffs
Western Virginia
July 28, 1862

I was sent out about a mile from camp to guard the premises of a citizen and although he has taken an oath to support the constitution of the Southern Confederacy and refuses to take the oath of allegiance, has been in the rebel army and is an avowed secessionist, yet we had orders not to let anyone take an apple out of his orchard or disturb anything about his premises. I suppose he would be in the rebel army at this time had he not been disabled by sickness. I have no hopes of a speedy termination of this war unless a different policy is resorted to by the Government.

While I was there, a Union man that had been taken prisoner by the rebels came and asked to stay with him overnight. He had voted against the ordinance of secession and had expressed his opinion in favor of the Union, which was all they accused him of and although he was 70 years old, while retreating from Lewisburg they took him to Union as a prisoner where he with sixteen others succeeded in making their escape. He was once wealthy but they took everything from him. He intends to stay here a few days until his wife can join him when they will go to some place of security. He was refused the privilege of staying all night and I directed him to camp where he could stay with some of the soldiers. I saw another man

Early in the war, departmental commanders felt obliged to enforce the letter of the fugitive slave act and would require runaway slaves found in camp to be delivered up to loyal citizens who claimed them. This policy caused distrust among the volunteer citizen army who looked upon it as a policy sympathetic to the Southern cause. Congress repealed the act in 1864. [6]

that was taken prisoner at the same time and for the same offense and had escaped at the same time who was also waiting for his wife to join him. She was obliged to leave home to escape being taken prisoner for selling some butter to some Union soldiers who were passing her house. There are numerous other cases of a similar character that I could mention if necessary.

The troops here are very well satisfied that General Pope has taken command of this division and also with the orders he has issued. Soldiers always prefer a general that has a firm and well defined purpose and one that believes in using every means to crush the rebellion.

For the benefit of those who are always harping about abolitionism, I will relate a circumstance that occurred yesterday. A man supposed to be loyal came into camp, claimed a negro that he said had run off from him and got permission of the General to take him home. The negro was not willing to go and so he procured some chains with which he tied his arms behind him and tied a long strap to the chain and drove him out of camp with a rawhide. None but Union men are allowed to do this...

It is so that we had to shed our lines to cross Greenbrier. Although I was not in the boat, I was an eyewitness of the scene and took a hearty laugh over it. As to the bees, although I was not stung, I had some hard fighting to do and the next man to me was stung in two places.

A detachment from the 44th and 36th of about 600 men have since made a reconnaissance out to the river and found that the rebels had constructed a second island No. 10 to command the ford by building fortifications and placing two cannon on an island just above the ford. It is held by about 1,000 rebels. I expect our next scout will be to try them a rub.

We have been reenforced by the Ninth Virginia Regiment, which is the poorest regiment I ever saw. Although it has been in the service as long as we have, they are ignorant of many of the most common principles of soldiery.

Mother thinks it must be very tiresome traveling so much. It is very tiresome sometimes, but I would rather take a tramp occasionally than to lay in one camp so long. When volunteers are asked for to take a tramp, a great many more always volunteer than are wanted. As long as I have good health, I

The Regimental Flag

On July 30th Colonel Gilbert acknowledged receipt of a new regimental flag, apparently a present from the sutler. Special Order No. 23 states:

"G.L. Houston, Sutler, having presented the splendid and costly regimental flag which we have on parade this evening to the regiment, I take pleasure in thus signifying our acceptance of the same and returning the thanks of the regiment to him.

"The spirit of good feeling thus evinced is the result of that strict sense of justice and liberality that has characterized your mutual intercourse which is equally honorable to all concerned.

"The beautiful symbols of our Nation's Glory which it bears on its azure folds should endear it to every patriotic heart and cause every soldier to feel as though he would yield the last spark of his life before he would allow it to be dishonored." [7]

Later, after leaving the service, Colonel Gilbert would be presented with the regimental flag by the officers and men of the 44th stating, "To your keeping we entrust this relic of the past, believing that you will prize it as we do the memory of our brave leader."

In its collection of Civil War flags, the Ohio Historical Society possesses one for the 44th Ohio Volunteer Infantry.

would as leave march half the time as to be around the camp. My feet never got sore but once when my shoes gave out. You thought I would not be able to stand marching, but I am counted the healthiest man in the company and can stand as much marching as anyone in it.

Meadow Bluffs
Western Virginia
July 9, 1862
(August 9, 1862)

I am on guard today guarding cattle and as I have not much to do, I thought I would write you a letter.

I have seen some pretty hot work. Last Saturday at 4 p.m., companies G, K and F were ordered to be ready to march in light marching orders at sundown, at which time we started in the direction of Haines Ford across Greenbrier River which is sixteen miles from here where we expected to find a small force of rebels.

We took the pike as far as Blue Sulphur Springs 6 miles from here where we took to the mountains where a great part of the way we had no path at all. It was either up or down hill all the way. It was very stony too, and so steep in some places that a horse could not climb up. Add to this almost pitch darkness and you will have some kind of an idea of the difficulties we had to surmount.

One of the boys near me said he would not mind climbing the hills so much if it were not for wading knee-deep in stones.

If we had not had the best guide in the country along, we would never have found the way. As it was essential that we should not be found out by anyone that would carry the intelligence to the rebels (which was our idea for taking the woods) we were ordered to not speak louder than a whisper. We marched in this manner making no noise, except when someone would lose his footing and fall ten or fifteen feet down the side of a mountain until he would lodge against a tree, until daylight when we halted to rest and breakfast for two hours. We resumed our march and at four o'clock came in sight of the river and the rebel camp on the other side.

Here we halted and concealed ourselves in the woods and sent the first platoon of Co. F out to reconnoiter. They came across two cavalry who had come across the river on a visit and took them prisoners. We then fell back a mile and laid by until morning when we crossed the river below the camp and intended to take them by surprise.

But instead of taking them by surprise (one or two hundred as we thought) we run into a trap set by between 500 and 700 rebels composed of one company of Thurmond's Moccasin Rangers, four companies 8th Virginia Cavalry and three companies 22nd Virginia Infantry. We were surrounded on three sides and if they had not been great cowards they would have closed in on us and taken or killed nearly all of us.

Company G, being in the lead, stood all the fire of the whole force about 15 minutes before the others were brought up. We fought until we found we could do nothing with them in their position when we fell back a quarter of a mile to a better position. We waited about an hour until, finding we could not draw them out of their position, we fell back across the river and halted about two hundred yards from it to rest.

After we had been there awhile they came down the side of the mountain and commenced bushwhacking across the river. Company K was sent to the river to deploy as skirmishers and Company G poured three volleys into them which pretty well settled them. We stayed here about four hours and started for camp.

Our second lieutenant was wounded in the thigh and B. Penny, from near Jaysville, in the arm. Our first lieutenant had his sword struck with a spent ball. There were a great many other narrow escapes. The balls passed very close on either side of me.

General Crook hearing that we were surrounded by a superior force sent the balance of the 44th and the 36th to our aid but when they got out the rebels had skedaddled as they always do when we have anything like equal numbers with them. The rebel loss is six killed and several wounded. It seems almost miraculous that we escaped so well but I suppose it is due in part to the efficiency of our arms and drill.

A great many of the rebels had shotguns and squirrel rifles with which they could not do much execution at long range.

In my last letter, I spoke of a man who would not take the oath. General Pope's order has fetched him to his senses. On the very day the orders came in force General Crook gave him the privilege of taking the oath or being taken outside the lines.

After fretting about it nearly all day, he at last consented to take the oath.

> Hawk's Nest
> Western Virginia
> August 17, 1862

Last Friday in the afternoon we received orders to draw and cook two days' rations immediately. The next morning, we started for this place where we arrived yesterday at noon. Our brigade is now nine miles from Gauley, and Cox is there with his force. It is rumored we will stay here until relieved by new regiments when we will go to the Shenandoah Valley, but as this is only a rumor I cannot vouch for the truth of it.

The rebels in front of us at Union and Greenbrier had nearly all left to reinforce Jackson at Gordonsville. As we could not advance from where we were on account of transportation, we fell back to this place. I think it is the policy to not make any offensive operations from this point but guard it with new regiments while the old ones are put into active service.

As I suppose you have often heard of Hawk's Nest, a description of the place will be interesting to you. It takes its name from being a cliff some eight hundred feet high. On looking over it, you see New River appearing straight down from where you stand. Yet, the best of throwers cannot cast a stone into the river and, although owing to the distance it looks like quite a small stream, yet a musket will not carry a ball to the opposite bank. The road runs along the edge of the cliff and at one time it was the situation of a large military camp. We are stationed a half mile from the cliff.

An incident occurred yesterday that occasioned some excitement among the boys. The brigade halted to rest, and one of our company who was sitting on a stone heard a hissing noise under him but thought nothing of it until he arose when a large rattlesnake made his appearance and was killed by the boys. I did not get to see it and have not seen one since I have been in the state.

I suppose the draft laws still occasion a great deal of excitement in the North. It meets with universal approbation with those now in the service as each one knows some coward at home that he would like to see drafted.

Camp
Western Virginia
August 30, 1862

Last Monday, our company received orders to draw five days' rations and be ready to march at 7 a.m., at which time we started for Carnifix Ferry which is sixteen miles from here. On reaching a good place to camp an hour before night within two miles of the ferry, we concluded to bivouac for the night. In reaching the ferry the next morning, we found that 300 rebels had crossed there at about three in the morning. They were citizens mostly from counties bordering on the Ohio River, and is thought some were from Ohio. They passed themselves off for Union men until they were outside of our liens when they told they were going to Staunton to join a regiment of rebel cavalry that is being raised at that place. On arriving near our advance lines, they burnt two government wagons and captured the teamsters and horses. They done this about four miles from Carnifix Ferry and near Cross Lanes.

After doing this, they were in such a hurry to get across the river that we found a good many trophies they had lost in the haste and confusion of crossing after night, among which was one horse that had given out, one squirrel rifle, a lot of cartridges, caps, etc. Had we went to the river to camp, we would have trapped the whole gang, which we would have done had we the least idea of what was going to happen. Here also, we learned that our orders were to blockade every road and bridlepath between that place and camp, which we done by felling large trees across them which made a very effectual blockade as we selected places where the roads run along the sides of hills where it is impossible to go around without cutting a new road, which is as much trouble as to build that much railroad in Ohio. The idea was not so much to keep out the rebels as to keep the citizens from running their stock off to the rebel army. The citizens through that country have from ten to fifteen miles to go to mill and many of them cannot possibly get a horse one mile from their houses. They were informed that if they opened any road or path or made any path around the blockade they would be driven from the country and all their property confiscated. This looks hard, but such are the consequences of war.

We spent five days in this kind of work and arrived in

camp yesterday evening. Other companies were sent in different directions for the same purpose so that the roads in fifteen or twenty miles are blockaded except a few which were left open for military operations.

The third day we were out, getting rather short of sowbellie the lieutenant told me to get two men and try to get some mutton for dinner. We started about 7 a.m. The first farmer we met had some sheep but they were in the mountains and could not be found. The next was the same and the next two the same until we came to the sixth where we found a man who had some sheep that were not running out. He said he had only sixteen and that was all he had to depend on for clothing for his family, but my instructions were to get the sheep wherever they could be found and I told him he would have to show me where they were. After hunting a half hour we seen them at a distance but they were as wild as deers and we could not get near them. Finding it impossible to drive them, one of the men succeeded in shooting one of them but that scared them so that we could not get close enough to shoot any more. So we gave the man the hide for dressing it and a note on Uncle Sam for $2.00 payable at the close of the war on conditions his loyalty can be proven.

Throwing our game across a pole, we started for the company where we arrived after they had been done eating their dinner some time. The sheep was small and when divided around made about a smell for each one. The cooks made soup of it and the boys in referring to it say they had a supper of scared water and bones.

I wrote you there was a probability of us going to the Shenandoah, but I suppose it is a settled matter that we will stay here for the present. The boys are all very much dissatisfied as they would rather went with the 36th, and a great many of the 36th swore they would lay down their arms if the 44th was not allowed to follow them. I understand since that their officers had a great deal of trouble to get them away. I never saw two regiments that had as much confidence in each other as the 44th and 36th. It seems as though to put the two together they fear nothing.

Tompkins Farm
Western Virginia
September 6, 1862

We have made another move. Last Thursday we received order to pack up and start at 8 a.m., at which time we started in the direction of Gauley and arrived at this place in the afternoon — a distance of eight miles. We are within two miles of Gauley Bridge. Here we found our tents ready for us and last night I enjoyed the luxury of sleeping in a tent for the first time in four months.

There are a great many reports afloat in regard to our future destination. Some say we will join General Cox in the Shenandoah; others that we will go to Kentucky; some that we are to hold the head of the Kanawha. A report was started this morning that the rebels have possession of the Kanawha below us and cut off our supplies. If so, you will probably not get this. There is one thing certain, that is they are shipping the large lot of supplies from Gauley down the river — how far, I don't know — probably to Charleston where we will fall back to and hold the valley from that point.

I suppose you have seen it reported in the papers that Bragg is about making for this valley; if he does, he will go through it as Cox took all the troops with him but the 34th, 37th and 44th Ohio and the 4th Virginia. But, I think we will be reinforced or probably relieved by green regiments before long.

An alarm was raised this morning at 3 a.m., and we were called into line. But after waiting a half hour, we were dismissed and piled into our bunks. The alarm was caused by a dispatch that a cavalryman brought in who was on a scout. I have not learned the nature of the dispatch.

The recruits have not arrived yet. It is reported they are at Charleston awaiting a move on our part in that direction.

In August, part of the Union forces in western Virginia was sent to reinforce the Army of Virginia and to participate later in the Antietam campaign, leaving only two brigades, including the 44th Ohio, in the Kanawha Valley. General Lee, upon learning of this movement, ordered Major General W.W. Loring to take advantage of this situation to invade western Virginia. Facing a large rebel force, the Union troops were forced to withdraw from the valley, the retreat being covered by the 44th, and were sent to Kentucky. Following the Antietam campaign, Union forces returned from the East and regained control of western Virginia. The 44th Ohio was, however, destined to spend the next year in the state of Kentucky.[8]

On September 19, 1862, the *Springfield Republic* reported, a private letter being its source, that "the 44th Ohio Regiment was in the movement down the Kanawha. It was attacked at its camp near Gauley Bridge and fought vigorously, but the force against it was four to one, and it was obliged to fall back. It retreated in fighting order holding the rebels in check. Its loss was small — the 44th left the Kanawha and marched to Pomeroy, Ohio, and was then transported to Point Pleasant where it now is." [9]

On October 11th, the following order was issued: "Colonel Samuel A. Gilbert, 44th Ohio Volunteers, will proceed with his regiment now at Point Pleasant, Western Virginia, to Covington, Kentucky, and report for duty to Major General Gordon Granger, U.S. Vols., Commanding the Army of Kentucky." [10]

Although remaining pro-slavery in sentiment, the Commonwealth of Kentucky did not choose to join the secessionist movement, but rather tried to remain neutral at the beginning of the war. Its roots were deep-seated in loyalty to the Union, as evidenced by the fact the state's electoral ballots in the 1860 election were cast for John Bell, the Constitutional Union candidate for President.[11] Kentucky's late U.S. senator, Henry Clay, the "Great Compromiser," had always championed loyalty to the Union as paramount to that for the state, although he had a strong attachment to the rights of the state.[12]

Congressional election in June of 1861 and state legislative elections held in August of the same year strengthened the Union position. There was no doubt that the prevailing sentiment in the state by late summer in 1861 was Unionist. Neutrality was over, with Federal forces moving in to establish positions in Paducah, at the mouth of the Tennessee River; Smithland at the mouth of the Cumberland; Louisville and Covington. Confederate forces from Tennessee occupied Columbus. Both sides continued to strengthen these positions. Late in the year Confederate sympathizers established a provisional government at Bowling Green, and by that vehicle Kentucky was admitted into the Confederacy. However, following the battles of Fort Henry on the Tennessee River and Fort Donelson on the Cumberland River, just south of the boundary between Tennessee and Kentucky, Confederate troops were forced to withdraw from their positions in Kentucky, and that state was in complete control of the Union forces by early 1862.

Kentucky experienced the first of John Hunt Morgan's raids in July 1862, followed by invasions by two major armies, commanded by Kirby Smith and Braxton Bragg, which resulted in the battles of Richmond in late August and Perryville in October. This effort was the high water mark of the Confederacy in Kentucky, and the Confederate forces returned south to Tennessee. However, John Hunt Morgan continued to make forays into his home state.[13]

Covington, Kentucky
October 17, 1862

We have changed our field of operations for one that I think will be a little more desirable than the Kanawha Valley. We received orders four days ago to draw six days' rations and be ready to march in two hours. We marched to Portland, the nearest railroad station, and came from there by rail. We marched through Cincinnati and Covington yesterday in the afternoon, and were enthusiastically cheered by all we passed.

We are now encamped in the suburbs of Covington, Kentucky, and are busy striking our tents. How long we will stay here or what our future movements will be of course we know nothing about. There is a considerable force here although I have no idea of the exact number.

I would like to see some of you down here. There is no telling how soon I will get home, but it will not be until winter sets in at best.

Morgan's Cumberland Gap army is on its way to Point Pleasant except one brigade which is here.

Covington, Kentucky
October 18, 1862

I wrote you that I wanted some of you to come here on a visit, and, as we have orders to leave tomorrow morning, I write this in hopes you will receive it in time to not come here with the intention of seeing me. I do not know where we are going to but the general impression is that our destination is Lexington, Kentucky, as 6 or 8 regiments have left here in that direction in the last few days.

The order has come rather unexpectedly as we expected to remain here several weeks to rest. I think our march will not be very long as we only draw two days' rations. With this, I will close for the present as I only intended to prevent you from coming here with the expectation of finding me here.

P.S. The aspect of things has changed this morning. We have drawed five days' rations instead of two and it is now said that Lexington is taken and that we are going there. These are rumors, we leave in a few minutes.

Lexington, Kentucky
October 26, 1862

We have again set our tents and are now encamped at Lexington, Kentucky. We started from Covington one week ago today and, after marching 4 days (80 miles), we arrived at Georgetown, a place as large as Piqua. Here we stayed one day and then came to this place, 95 miles from Cincinnati.

We are encamped in sight of Henry Clay's monument. It is 100 feet high and is made of marble. It looks like an immense pillar of snow. It is situated in a cemetery among quite a number of small monuments making one of the nicest burial grounds I ever saw.

There is about 10 regiments camped here under command of General Gilmore. The rebels under John Morgan came here a week ago and captured 150 of the 10th Ohio cavalry. He paroled them on the spot. There was only 300 troops here at the time. The rest were secreted in houses by the citizens.

There is a great deal of Union sentiment here as well as every where we have been in the state. We were enthusiastically cheered all along the route, and flags were displayed at almost every house. There is some of the finest farm residences between here and Cincinnati I ever saw. The fences along the road are mostly stone, many of them set in masonry. The houses are mostly set back from the road two to three hundred yards with groves mostly of locusts to the road. It is only 12 miles to Frankfort, the capitol of the state.

P.S. R. Kent with a view to getting a furlough, has been telling that his wife is suffering for wood and that she cannot get it chopped at any price. Is it so? I do not believe it.

Lexington, Kentucky
November 4, 1862

One of our men who took a French furlough from

Covington and has returned, says he met Father coming to see us and when he heard we had started on a tramp that he went back. I regret very much that we did not stay longer at Covington. The persons he saw told him they had furloughs but it was a mistake. One of them (Danield Wineland) is in the guardhouse awaiting a courtmartial. He came back after being absent eight days. There was no furloughs granted at Covington. About fifty took French furloughs. Several have come back and are in the guardhouse awaiting a courtmartial.

Captain Newkirk is at Columbus on recruiting service. Our 1st Lieutenant (Shaw) has tendered his resignation on account of ill health and some difficulty that has arose in regard to furloughs; he has never received a furlough yet, and some pecuniary matters make it necessary to be at home by the 16th of this month or sustain a heavy loss.

Our recruits joined us last Friday. They are a good looking set of fellows. Harvey Bierly will be a drummer, Wesley a fifer and Daniel Eirsman in all probability will be a bugler.

You wrote as though you had some notion of enlisting. I don't think under the circumstances you are duty bound to go and if you were I have no idea you could stand it. Anyone who is weak in the breast has no business in the army. If you have any notions of enlisting, I would advise you to march 20 miles some day with a load of 40 lbs. and then stand guard 2 hours out of six the next night, and if you feel like marching 20 miles the next day, enlist in the first company you come across.

Father wants to know if I am company commissary or regimental commissary. I have charge of the company commissary. It has always been in charge of a sergeant until I took it.

We had snow four inches deep last week, but the weather is very nice now. I attended church in Covington last Sunday and will go tomorrow if I can get a pass.

Lexington, Kentucky
December 3, 1862

We had another Grand Review last Friday by General Granger accompanied by Major General Wright and Brigadier Generals Judah, Gillmore and Smith. There were out two brigades infantry (seven regiments), two batteries artillery and one regiment cavalry. I wish you could be present at one of these reviews. It is a grand sight to see a line of soldiers as far as you can see. But, it is very fatiguing to the men on account of having to stand a long time at shouldered arms without moving scarcely a muscle.

We have again resorted in part to the elementary rules of drilling. We drill 2 hours each day without arms and in the position of a soldier and the facings; we then drill four hours in the company and battalion drill.

Tell Mother that when we drawed our tents last spring we drawed stoves with them. Not needing them in summer, they were turned in and this fall not being sure whether we would get them replaced we bought sheet iron stoves costing $3.00 apiece. I have boards to lay on and sleep very nice. If mother has any provisions she would like to send, they would come very acceptable if sent soon. If you wait, we may get marching orders in which case I would not get them. They can be shipped by express with entire safety and will come in two days. Scipio Myers received a barrel of apples from home before he received a letter that was mailed the day before the apples were started. If you send anything, please pay the expressage as I am played out in the cash line. I had money when the recruits came, but as they were all strapped and I expecting to draw about the 15th of last month, I bought gloves, etc. that they needed, amounting to over 10 dollars. We were not paid at this time and will not be until we have four months coming to us, which will be about the 15th of next month. If you can spare $1.00 as handy as not, it would come good at present if you send it in change; that is, postage stamps, currency or anything in the way of change. Stamps are as good as silver here, and one cannot get a dollar changed without taking out about 60 cents. If you cannot spare it handy, I can get along very well without it.

Richmond, Kentucky
December 12, 1862

We have made another move, and, as it is my intention to keep you well posted in regard to our movements, I will give you an account of everything as it transpired that I think would be of interest to you.

We were called up last Wednesday morning at two a.m. and ordered to get breakfast and be ready to march by day-

light, at which time our brigade under command of Colonel Gilbert and accompanied by the 18th Ohio Battery started to go someplace but we did not know where.

The first night we encamped on the banks of the Kentucky River; the next morning we were awoke at 2 a.m. and marched down to the river. Here we found a small ferryboat large enough to take two wagons across at a time. As that was too slow a way to transport a brigade across, we only ferried the wagon across and the men went up the stream to a shallow place and forded it. We pulled our stockings off, leaving our shoes on, and rolled our britches above the knee. By winding around the shallow places, it was only half knee deep and two hundred yards wide. The river was covered with ice where it did not run too swiftly and, the morning being frosty, made it a rather cold bath.

After crossing, we marched a half mile and halted for breakfast. We were delayed here until about ten a.m. waiting for our train to cross. The wagons could only get to the river at the ferry and there it was too deep to ford.

At one p.m. of the second day, we arrived at Richmond where we have struck our tents but will probably move to the other side of town tomorrow.

We found here three regiments infantry and one battery artillery and one regiment cavalry. It is generally thought that no forward movement is intended from this point soon and that this will be our winter quarters. We are in sight of where the battle was fought last August. I have seen several horses laying with holes shot through them. There is also a graveyard near where many Union and rebel soldiers are buried. Many of the boys have been cutting bullets out of trees.

There is a fence near where it is said the rebels made three unsuccessful charges and were repulsed every time.

If you have not sent the box, I suppose you had better not send it at present. But if any of you intended coming down, we are only 26 miles further and the stage runs every day. The fare to Lexington is $2.00. Richmond is a county seat and is some larger than Greenville.

Danville, Kentucky
December 31, 1862
We have again been on the move and landed at this place last evening. We started from Richmond the day before yesterday at daylight. Our march was performed without anything occurring worthy of mention. But yesterday evening, a letter was intercepted which John Morgan had sent to his mother at Lexington stating that he was going to attack this place this morning. The letter was dated yesterday. We were aroused up last night at ten o'clock and ordered to sleep with our accoutrements on and our arms by our side. And in addition to that, each company was to furnish a man to be on guard all the time to awaken the company on the occasion of any alarm.

So confident were the commanders of an attack that we were all ordered up this morning before daylight, but I suppose Morgan who is always awake heard of our brigade coming and wisely desisted from attacking us up to this time (noon). He advanced to within fifteen miles last night when I suppose he heard of our arrival and is probably by this time demanding the surrender of some smaller detachment elsewhere.

In his third raid into Kentucky (the so-called Christmas Raid) John Hunt Morgan's two brigades entered the state near Tompkinsville and proceeded north to Elizabethtown and Bardstown. The raid succeeded in the disruption of services on the Louisville and Nashville Railroad, the capture of almost 2,000 Union troops, their arms and supplies and with very few Confederate casualties. Turning south before reaching Danville, Morgan's forces successfully bypassed Lebanon where Union troops were concentrated and by a series of forced marches, retreated safely from the state.

I am sorry Father did not get down to see us while at Richmond, but we are no further from Lexington. With railroad communication nearly all the way, if he is still in the notion of coming tell him to come via Lexington and Nicholsville from which place there is a stage running to this place.

Danville is nearly as large as Piqua and is the finest town for the size I have ever seen. It contains the finest female symmetry I have seen anywhere. It is also a very aristocratic town. As aristocracy and negroes go together, of course the town fairly swarms with slaves. They are seen standing in squads of ten to thirty on every corner.

I was offered the position of quartermaster's secretary which is a splendid position. The pay is 25 cents per day extra, but to be that it would be necessary to be reduced to ranks and the lieutenant has refused to permit me to go to the ranks as I am the ranking corporal and he wants me to receive the next promotion. Our second lieutenant said if I would not go to the ranks I would be a sergeant before a month as our orderly would be promoted to a lieutenant. Notwithstanding, if I can get the position of secretary, I will take it in preference to a promotion. A quartermaster's secretary has nothing to do but to write, has no gun, no knapsack to carry and it is a nice position.

At his own request Corporal McKee was reduced to ranks to accept the position of commissary clerk, a position he held as a private for the remainder of his enlistment.

Correspondent Zouave wrote to the *Springfield Republic* on January 2, 1863, summarizing the activities of the regiment in withdrawing from the Kanawha Valley, the move to Kentucky and the pursuit of John Hunt Morgan. His report was published on January 9, 1863:

"The gallant 44th has undergone many trials since your correspondent was permitted to be with it. We left it at Meadow Bluff. From thence it was ordered East with the Kanawha Division, and fully expected to be part of the army of the Potomac, till it reached Camp Ewing and received the order substituting the 28th Ohio for the 44th, and ordering it to guard the valley. Shortly after, warned by scouts and the sound of the enemy's cannon at Fayetteville, it prepared for the memorable retreat down the valley. I have been informed that although not mentioned in the telegraphic accounts of the retreat, it under Colonel Gilbert, performed the skillful and daring feats of the retreat. The reason of the omission was that after the retreat, while each regiment was represented in Gallipolis by commissioned officers who took care to expatiate on the part performed by their regiments, all the officers of the 44th were with their commands. The 44th checked the enemy at Montgomery's Ferry and held them at bay while Col. Seiber hurried the exhausted companies of the 34th and 37th down the left bank of the Kanawha. It then covered the retreat down the right bank of the river to Charleston, a distance of 38 miles with masses of cavalry and infantry constantly thundering at its heels, but the lines were never broken. If pushed too close, the boys were ordered to stand, the artillery concealed behind a bend, and then by a skillful falling back they brought the enemy in close range only to drive them back in confusion after a few volleys. Col. Gilbert was the master spirit of the occasion. At Charleston, the 47th was left in the city to act as skirmishers. The other regiments were in position on the opposite side of the Elk River. The rebels were pouring in their masses, when a messenger came to Col. Lightburn, to know if the 47th should fall back. Col. Lightburn was uncertain what to order, when Col. Gilbert advised that they should be ordered back, or five minutes would see them prisoners. The order was given, and sure enough, the regiment was saved by a few minutes. During the fiercest of the engagement, the Colonel rode along the line of skirmishers distributing cartridges from a full haversack. A squad of cavalry coming under a sharp artillery fire began to light out. He stopped them with, 'Don't be running down there on my men. They have been shooting at me all day, and can't hit me.'

"At 2 o'clock things looked dark, and Col. Lightburn wanted to destroy the immense train of 720 wagons, but Col. Gilbert was unwilling and determined on seeing it out. An hour afterwards, the Colonel seeing that the train hadn't started, rode back, and with a 'why in the h--l hasn't this train started,' demanded an explanation of the train master. Colonel Lightburn, who happened to overhear him, spoke up and said that he had been unable to start them. Says Gilbert, 'I'll be d--d if I can't,' and rode to the head of the train. In fifteen minutes the train was in motion and saved.

"The rebels were playing on the boys all day with 30 guns. At dark Major Mitchell told them that now they must face the cold iron, and the retreating commenced again. Unfortunately, a barn had been fired toward the close of the engagement, and it lit up the road clearly for a great distance. The regiment had to march a mile, while the rebel guns volleyed and thundered on them. It did it, and at common time. Not a man lost his place or the step, and when the shells would burst around them without effect, the boys would hurl back their taunts at the rebel gunners.

"From Point Pleasant the regiment was ordered to Lexington, Kentucky, where the new recruits joined them.

"At Lexington, the 44th was assigned to the 2nd Brigade, and Col. Gilbert assumed command of the brigade.

"Amid the comforts of Lexington, we felt like militia on a muster, and the veterans of the 44th were glad to be ordered to Richmond. The march was pleasant and weather superb. The fortifications at Richmond were finished, and all had set down for the winter, when an order came to the 2nd Brigade to move to Danville, to assist in capturing Morgan, who was reported to be everywhere.

"The country presented the same everlasting hilly aspect, the weather good. The night we arrived at Danville, Morgan was expected. His spies had gone out the day before we arrived and as he announced his determination in an intercepted letter to capture Danville and was unaware of our reinforcement, and was being driven this way and citizens reported his advance. General Bain and Uncle Sammy, as the boys called Colonel Gilbert, increased their usual precautions. No fires were to be seen anywhere, no noises could be heard, the men slept on their arms, the plan of battle was arranged and we awaited John; but morning came and no Morgan. He or any other rebel may whip the 2nd Brigade, but can never surprise it; for our Colonel's eyes are everywhere. Our camp is in a beautiful grassy meadow. How long we will remain is for the powers that be to determine. Lieutenant Colonel Wilson is in command of the regiment, and becomes more of a soldier every day.

"We hope the President will increase his good appointments by adding Colonel Gilbert to the Constellation of Brigadiers."

1863

OHIO

1863

Frankfort, Kentucky
January 7, 1863

We have again been on the march, and I hasten to write you a few lines to let you know where we are. We left Danville last Monday morning and arrived at this place today at noon, a distance of 42 miles. If Father still intends coming to see us, now is his chance. There is direct railroad communications with Cincinnati. I cannot tell what the fare is as we just arrived today.

In my last letter, I spoke of getting a position. I have been appointed Regimental Commissary Clerk. It is a splendid position. I have nothing to do but to keep the quartermaster accounts, and on a march I have all my things hauled and can ride part of the time if I wish to. My wages are 40 cents per day extra, which with my regular wages makes $25.00 per month. If Father comes down, tell him to be sure to bring my silver holder as I will have to get one.

You may wonder why we came here. I will tell you. The Kentucky State Legislature meets here tomorrow and it is said that we are to stay here during the session. I was very much disappointed in my expectations of finding a nice town here. It is the ugliest town I have seen in Kentucky. It is in a hollow surrounded by high barren river bluffs.

I saw a rather novel sight yesterday. It was a young lady of about 18 who had dressed in men's clothes and joined the rebel army. She had got into our lines and stolen a horse from the man that raised her and was making for Rebeldom when she was taken prisoner for stealing when she was found out. She is in the Frankfort jail. When dressed in men's clothes, she made a good appearance and looked like a delicate boy of 17 or 18 years.

*Camp near Frankfort,
Kentucky
(no date)*

After so long a silence, I have at last received your kind letter of the 6th which arrived several days ago and would have been answered sooner had it not been that the mail was stopped on account of the snow which obstructed the railroad tracks for nearly a week so that we could neither send nor receive mail. We have had a rough time of it for the last two weeks. First, it rained almost constantly for two days. This was followed by a three days snow, rain and sleet. Then succeeded several days of cold weather and now the snow is going off with a drenching rain. But, I have nothing to complain of as I have no guard or other outdoor duty to perform.

I am getting along very well in my new position and like it better every day. I think it is the business I was destined for, and tell Father I want him to have a good situation selected for me as a bookkeeper or clerk when the war ends. There is no better business in the world than this to learn bookkeeping. Here everything is subjected to a rigid scrutiny, first by the commander of the regiment, and then by the brigade quartermaster and commander of the brigade. If any mistakes occur or blots are seen, they are thrown back on our hands.

Last Monday morning, our brigade was ordered to reinforce General Rosecrans but at 10 a.m. it was countermanded and General Baird's division went in our stead. It is very currently reported in camp that our regiment is to be mounted and act as mounted infantry.

Our lieutenant colonel is absent somewhere, and it is said he has gone to get the horses. I give you this as a doubtful rumor and you can place as much confidence in it as you like.

Has Father given up coming to see us altogether, or will he be down? I am very anxious to see some of you. Our first lieutenant (Shaw) went home several days ago on detached service to hunt up deserters. He lives in Greenville. Father may get to see him. If he does, he will find him a very gentlemanly soldier and can have an interesting talk with him. He has been in command of the company for about six months and is very well liked by all. But the company are all bitter in their *enunciation against Captain Newkirk, and it is currently reported that he has been requested to resign by Colonel Gilbert. He makes a good appearance of caring for his men but it is only the cloak that covers his selfish designs. But in Lieutenant Shaw we have always found a gentleman as well as a good officer.*

I am sorry to hear of mother's illness but hope she is well by this time. I wish she had a half bushel of our crackers. They are very wholesome.

I have just heard from Colonel Gilbert's secretary that the requisition has been made out for horses to mount our regiment and you need not be surprised if it is the case. I think it will do very well in the summer but I would not fancy it in the winter.

I received the dollar in postage stamps enclosed in your letter. I did not need it as bad as when I wrote some time ago as we have been paid off. As it is said we will not be paid off until the 15th of March, I will not send any home this time.

*Frankfort, Kentucky
February 6, 1863*

You and mother will please accept my warmest thanks for the rich treat of provisions you were so kind to send. The puddings were fine, the chicken excellent and, in fact, everything was got up in a style that betokened a high appreciation of a soldier's appetite for dainties. Tell Aunt Margaret I am a thousand times obliged to her for the fine fruit cake she was so kind as to send and tell her it seems to me there was a striking contrast between it and the kind of cakes Uncle Sam's bakers prepare for us. Tell Mary, Loula, Estelle and Edwin I send them each a kiss for the fine apples they enclosed for me. I think of them very often and hope Mary will soon be able to write.

We are still here with no prospect of a move and everything is going on in the old way. There are rumors every day of Morgan or some other scallawag coming here to attack us but no one pays any attention to them. Our regiment and the 104th Ohio had orders several days ago to cook three days' rations and be ready to march at a half hour's notice, but the order to leave was never given and we are still here. The order was only for a scout as we were to leave our tents and commissary stores.

I approve very much of your plan of studying algebra while reviewing arithmetic. One will help along with the other. I believe I have an algebra book somewhere. If you can find it, it will answer your purpose. I would also advise you to spend your spare time in reading. Read something if it is nothing but novels. I would not encourage the reading of novels probably against your inclinations and father's wishes, but in the absence or disinclination to read anything else they will learn you to exert your reasoning faculties and thereby aid you in composition and delivery in speech — but I am growing tedious and will close for the present.

> *Frankfort, Kentucky*
> *February 21, 1863*

We have been very busy for some time issuing horses and equipment, but at last we are through and the 44th Ohio Volunteer Mounted Regiment or O.V.M.I. takes the place of the O.V.I. We have as a general thing very good horses notwithstanding there are many poor ones among them. I had choice from the whole regiment and have a nice little black. I have been training him to jumping logs and fences and am succeeding finely. He will jump over almost any log now.

To give you an idea of what it takes to support an army, I will tell you what our horses consume in one day. The ration is fourteen pounds of hay and 12 pounds of corn per day for each horse, which for the regiment makes an aggregate of 8-1/2 tons of hay and 171 bushels of corn.

No doubt you have read an account of the Butternut convention that tried to meet here this week. That morning our regiment was ordered to saddle and be ready to march at a moment's notice. Our saddles were kept on all day, guns cleaned out and the boys were just aching to go down and fix them like Paddy did the Hessians; viz., surround them. A rumor was started that Vallandingham was there, and it was immediately agreed upon to address a note signed by all the 44th requesting him to leave in short notice or bear consequences which would be nothing short of ropes in my opinion. He may have some few friends in the regiment, but if there is any they are obliged to keep very dark.

The Butternut Convention to which John McKee refers was a

meeting of Democratic delegates that were dispersed by the Federal forces occupying the city. They were attempting to organize and nominate candidates for state election in opposition to the loyal Unionists in control of state government. As soon as the convention was called to order and the roll taken, Colonel Gilbert addressed the meeting as follows:

"I hope no one in this house will create any disturbance, or utter any seditious sentiments, as it will compromise the whole assemblage, and possibly lead to your arrest.

"No doubt, gentlemen have assembled here without any treasonable design, either present or prospective. All such I invite to retire peaceably and quietly to their homes. There are those here whom we know to be rebels of the worst kind — the great plotters of treason — who, to carry out their infamous designs, would deluge the fair fields of Kentucky in the blood of her citizens and make her rich plantations, beautiful villages and wealthy cities as desolate as are the domains of the Southern traitors with whom they are in league.

"Under the guise of that good old name — Democrat — they hope to perfect their designs; but it will not do. You are repudiated by this conservative Democratic Legislature, in the refusal of their house for the holding of your meeting. The Democratic newspapers scorn and disown you. Democrats in high places and in low places, call your leaders by the one name — TRAITORS!

"There is no use in your holding Conventions in Kentucky, as none but men of undoubted loyalty to the United States Government will, under any circumstances, be allowed to run for any office, or to fill it if elected. Such meetings as this you shall not hold within the limits of my command; and to avoid difficulty, you will disperse to your homes, and in the future desist from all such attempts to precipitate civil war upon your State." [1]

Upon Colonel Gilbert's insistence that the meeting should disperse, a motion to adjourn was carried. The local newspaper commenting on the events that took place stated that, acting under the information Colonel Gilbert had, he did precisely right, and as any United States officer placed in his position was bound to do. [2]

There was a strong resentment to Colonel Gilbert's actions in dispersing a political party's convention. However, the military continued to interfere with the political process in Kentucky to assure that those who held office were not in support of the rebellion.³

Clement L. Vallandingham was an outspoken critic of the Lincoln Administration and of the war effort. A former congressman from Ohio, having been defeated in 1862 for reelection, he became "the spokesman for the irritated and disaffected people. He expressed himself with great boldness of utterance, denounced the war, denounced the draft, stirred up the people with violent talk and particularly excited them and himself over alleged efforts on the part of the military authorities to interfere with freedom of speech and of the press —." He was soon to be arrested, tried by military tribunal and imprisoned pursuant to orders of General Ambrose Burnside. He shortly thereafter was ordered released from prison and placed in exile beyond enemy lines by President Lincoln. A candidate for the Ohio governorship in 1863, Vallandingham was soundly defeated by Republican John Brough.

John Brough's candidacy was to receive the endorsement of the men of the 44th or, as correspondent Zouave wrote to the *Springfield Republic*: "The 'soger boys' nominate John Brough for governor by acclamation. Put the man on the track that will beat Vallandingham. For God's sake, don't permit Ohio to be disgraced, and cause her sons to blush by his election."

In March 1863 at a meeting of prominent citizens of Springfield, a resolution was adopted praising Colonel Gilbert and as a token of their "admiration of his fidelity in executing whatever has been assigned him," and in suppressing disloyalty within his lines, money was raised and a fine horse was purchased and presented to the Colonel. Both the resolutions and the Colonel's lengthy response were published in the *Springfield Republic* on April 3, 1863. Colonel Gilbert, defending his action at Frankfort, stated: "We of the Army look with suspicion upon those sticklers for a strict adherence to form and rules not made in anticipation of the present condition of things; and we denounce as traitors, those who refuse to so amend laws and rules as to make them fit the emergencies forced upon us; thereby embarrassing and delaying us in the field. We do not think they have any right to claim the benefits of the Government they are seeking to enjoy.

"For the horse you have my hearty thanks. He is indeed a splendid animal, and I will take pleasure in using him in the service for which he was intended by the donors."

I think I informed you that we're going to have a brass

band in place of the one we used to have. Their horses came today, and the band will be organized immediately. The members are all to have grey horses in accordance with the army regulations. I believe I called it a brass band but they have silver instruments.

Since writing, the regiment has started on a scout somewhere and I am left in charge of the Q.M. stores.

Richmond, Kentucky
March 14, 1863

Our regiment has been scouting all over Kentucky for the past month, however, I was left at Frankfort in charge of the Quartermaster's papers and remained there until four days ago when I was ordered to join the regiment at this place.

I was very sorry to leave Frankfort as I had found the acquaintance of quite a number of the belles of the place and was just beginning to enjoy myself when I was ordered to join the regiment.

I attended several parties there, and, as it may be of interest to you to know how a party is conducted, I will give you a programme of the second party I attended. It was late when I arrived, and I found quite a number present who were amusing themselves at playing cards. Of course, they invited me to take a hand with them. Both from necessity and choice, I respectfully declined. After the guests had all arrived, card playing was dispensed with for awhile and plays were introduced similar to those used in Ohio. After playing some time, a little darkie appeared bearing a tray on which was wine and glasses. We drank health to Lincoln, Gilbert, etc., while some of the ladies toasted Jeff Davis. One of the ladies who had a brother in each army said she had often tried to be for the Union but found it impossible.

After refreshments came dancing. I declined at first on the grounds that I had never danced, but they did not deem this a sufficient excuse and insisted that I should take the floor. At last a little curly-headed vixen volunteered to learn me how and insured me to be successful. I consented and they say I done excellent. You may think this a curious programme for a party, but it is the custom here among the best class of society. The ladies that were there were many of them Presbyterians and were of the most respectable class. I don't suppose any of *them would have attended a promiscuous ball such as are so common in the North where none are invited but all are welcome who buy a ticket. They think the only harm there is in dancing is the excess to which it is sometimes carried and company present.*

Several companies of the regiment started on a scout today. Our regiment had several unimportant skirmishes during the late raid but none worth mentioning.

On March 27, Correspondent Zouave reported:

"To write the history of the 44th since it has been mounted would require a multitude of historians. At present it is divided into three detachments. One at Paris and Winchester, under Lieut. Col. Wilson; one at Hickman's Bridge, and one at Lexington. The last has been ordered to the Bridge and leaves tomorrow. A part of Col. Wilson's detachment, two hundred strong, fought six hundred rebels and whipped them. The enemy lost several killed and wounded. Our loss was two wounded —

"Several citizens who witnessed the skirmish were delighted with the manner of the 44th and are filling Lexington with praises of its coolness and gallantry.

"Lieut. J. Badger, at Hickman's Bridge, with four men, captured a rebel picket of fifteen men, and brought them in safely, though four hundred rebels were hundred yards distant.

"Col. Gilbert, much to his chagrin, has been appointed Commandant of Post, at Lexington. The detachment here remained behind for want of horses, but has since been mounted so far as Uncle Sam could do it, and tomorrow leaves for the front. Col. Gilbert expects to be relieved, and be with his brigade. There is a general movement forward.

"Col. Lightburn has been made a Brigadier General, for his masterly retreat out of the Kanawha Valley. Ask the men and officers who made the retreat, and saved the train, and see if they and Congress agree. That 'star' should glisten on Col. Gilbert's shoulder."

Mount Vernon, Kentucky
April 1, 1863

Since writing last, we have made two moves: from Lancaster to Crab Orchard where we stayed a week and yesterday we arrived at this place. You say the papers differ with me slightly in regard to the number of prisoners and cattle taken near Somerset. Our regiment escorted one hundred and ninety-nine prisoners to Lexington and I heard of a number of others taken to Wolford's men. As to cattle, there was some butchered at Somerset, and we took one hundred and forty-five to Danville. It is always hard to form a correct estimate of prisoners or anything else taken in battle when so many regiments are engaged. It is easy to know what is going on in one's own regiment or detachment, but outside of that it is very difficult to arrive at anything definite.

We have bid farewell to the best part of Kentucky and are now among the spurs of the Cumberland Mountains. Of course, the country is very poor and we are compelled to haul forage from twenty to twenty-five miles, but I think in about two more jumps we will be in Tennessee where forage will be more plenty.

A scouting party from our regiment has just arrived in camp that was within seven miles of the line. Another detachment of four companies started out this morning. The boys have no want of exercise as they are kept scouting nearly all the time.

While I write, our artillery is practicing at a target at the distance of three miles. They can throw a shell into a house at that distance about once out of four shots.

I sent Father some money by express a week ago and since that I have sent you a printed roll of our company. I suppose you have received both by this time.

I hope the conscript law will not take you, but if it does, get into the cavalry or gunboat or artillery service if you can or anything but infantry. This thing of marching twenty or twenty-five miles per day with a load of from twenty to forty pounds is no easy task. Our regiment has been envied by all the rest of the brigade since being mounted.

Our lieutenant colonel resigned and left us for Springfield while at Crab Orchard. He resigned partly on account of health and partly on account of having a large amount of business matter to settle at home. He raised the regiment, has been with it since its organization and will be greatly missed by the men.

I have been expecting a furlough and wanted to take you by surprise. As it is, I have a leave of absence for 20 days approved by the quartermaster, captain of the company, commander of regiment and commander of brigade. It is to *be approved by commander of division and commander of department, so you see it has run the gauntlet of four out of six of the red tape gentlemen and will probably be here the last of the week.*

Our company has been in sight of Cumberland Gap and is now at Barboursville.

One June 5, 1863, the Springfield citizens heard from their correspondent Zouave. His report, dated June 1, and as reported in the *Springfield Republic,* included the following:

"Lieutenant-Colonel Wilson has resigned. We could well have spared another. In energy, in procuring charges for the regiment he was unequaled. Wherever the Colonel goes, he carries with him the regards and best wishes of the regiment.

"Within the last two months the regiment has done an enormous amount of scouting and has made some bold dashes. An idea of the work may be gained from the fact that within the last month the 44th has drawn 460 horses. Over one-half of the horses of the regiment have been used up by one month's duty. The regiment is compelled to guard as much as is covered by six mounted regiments at Somerset. The men are in the saddle almost constantly. The horses are kept in a country destitute of forage, and by a Department Order are put on half rations. Is it any wonder then that horses are used up at the rate of $46,000 worth per month. In addition to guarding the country that has been and is now protected, Maj. Moore has had a skirmish at Red Bird, in which, with seventy men, he whipped three hundred rebels, with what loss to them is not known. Captain Stough routed them at Williamsburg, and to cap the climax, Captain Tulleys with a small force crossed the Cumberland and pushed on toward the Gap. He captured the rebel pickets, drove in their reserves and coolly rode in long musket range around their fortifications, while the rebels in tenfold force lay trembling behind them. After making a thorough reconnaissance the captain slowly retreated with his force. The rebels pursued, but overtaking the rear guard, they were punished severely and fell back, concluding they had caught a Tartar. As the boys were returning with their prisoners and captured horses, they found the following note:

" 'Compliments of the 6th Georgia Cavalry to the 44th Ohio Mounted Infantry. We believe you to be the foeman worthy of our steel. Will you fight us, swap horses with us or drink with us? Please answer by card posted within our lines.'

"Captain Badger endorsed the following reply on the back of the note: 'We are sorry that we can not return your compliments; and do not see how you should know us to be foremen worthy of your steel, as you have never stolen anything from us. We have given you many opportunities to fight us, but you have uniformly declined. As for swapping horses with you, we would say that we have taken liberty to exchange a few this evening. In regard to drinking, you know that we came to the Gap where we supposed you kept such delicacies, but you neglected to invite us. Finally, an insuperable objection to our acceding to either of your propositions exists in the fact that we endeavor to fight, swap horses and drink with gentlemen.' ...

"The 44th is now divided into several detachments. Headquarters are at London ... The 44th is campaigning this summer without tents. All that one has to see to is his horse. Arm the regiment with Colt's revolving carbine and pistols, and it will soon become a terror to more rebels than those between us and Knoxville."

London, Kentucky
June 2, 1863
We are packed up ready for a move and hasten to write you a few lines, not to tell you where we are going, but to tell you we are going somewhere but I haven't the least idea where that will be. We received orders last night to pack everything up for the purpose of sending to the rear, except one change of clothes. We have turned our tents in and will have none this summer. Except Wolford's 1st Kentucky Regiment, the 44th has done more scouting than any regiment in the state in the last two months.

The furlough has not come yet but will be good in three months if it does not come sooner. This move will probably detain it some time but it is none the less sure. You will wonder that it takes so long to get a furlough. The regulations provide that commanders of regiments can issue furloughs but our department commander is such a devotee to red tape that he has issued an order that they shall go up through the regular channel to him, making it a slow process.

The weather is getting very warm here, causing an increase of sickness. I have got along remarkably well, with the exception of a slight diarrhea for a few days.

Mount Vernon, Kentucky
June 25, 1863

We are still encamped at this place although the regiment has been scouting nearly all the time. Six companies have just returned from a raid into Tennessee. They went via Big Creek Gap and were across the line, a distance of 25 miles. The other four companies went on under command of General Carter in the direction of Knoxville. Company G is with this detachment. They have not been heard from for some time, and rumor has it they have been captured but I think it started from a rebel correspondence that appeared in the Commercial which said the rebels hoped to surround and capture them. That is a game that rarely succeeds and ere this reaches you the companies will in all probability have made their appearance in camp. Their intention in going so far into Tennessee was to destroy railroad and burn an important bridge.

The six companies that have returned had several unimportant skirmishes in Tennessee and took several prisoners but returned without any loss. They took six in one engagement near Pine Mountain in Tennessee.

I have been enjoying myself very well since we came here last. I have become acquainted with quite a number of the belles of the place. Some of them are well educated and possess a high degree of refinement. I was at two parties last week and, of course, enjoyed myself to the utmost.

We have arrangements made for an excursion to a cave on next Saturday. It is a salt peter cave, goes though a hill like a tunnel, is a mile long and is about eight miles from here. It is said to contain stalactites and is represented to be very beautiful and large enough for one to ride into on horseback.

It has been raining almost constantly for two days but has an appearance of clearing off, and I hope we will be favored with nice weather. The party is to consist of six couples. The adjutant's clerk and myself are the only soldiers that are going.

Our lieutenant colonel has resigned and started for home today. He was a splendid officer and will be sadly missed by the regiment. Major Moore is left in command and will probably be promoted to Lt. Colonel. He entered the service as captain of Company A and is noted only for tyranny and lack of judgment.

Since writing the above, the four companies spoken of have

been heard from. They had a skirmish in sight of Knoxville but as the rebs had 16 pieces of artillery and our men had no piece they declined going any further than the pickets. However, they tore up a great amount of railroad and burned a number of bridges. I have not heard of any loss on our side although I have not heard the particulars. You will see them in the papers nearly as soon as I will hear them.
It is still raining with little prospect of ceasing.

The four companies of the 44th, including Company G, were part of a mixed brigade of 1,500 cavalry and mounted infantry under command of Colonel William P. Sanders which was sent into eastern Tennessee to disrupt communications. Under leadership of the Kentucky-born West Pointer, the Union forces set out on June 14th and in the course of nine days succeeded in disrupting rebel communications and the destruction of several bridges along the vital Tennessee and Virginia Railroad, including a 1,600-foot bridge across the Holston River. The raid was a forerunner of the soon-to-come and long-anticipated invasion and "liberation" of eastern Tennessee by the army of the Ohio under command of Maj. General Ambrose E. Burnside.[5]

Hickman Bridge, Kentucky
July 9, 1863
I suppose you have heard of the present raid in Kentucky. Our regiment has fallen back from Mount Vernon to Stanford. The train is at Camp Dick Robinson and, as the other clerk went with the detachment, I am obliged to stay with the train which has been laying at Camp Dick Robinson waiting for orders. Today, I have come to this place to visit our company which has been here resting since the raid into Tennessee. We will in all probability be ordered to the advance soon unless the rebs reappear. I go back to the train this evening, but I have no more time to write now. All is activity here.

Stanford, Kentucky
July 15, 1863
I wrote you a few lines from Hickman's Bridge last week in which I said I was laying at Camp Dick Robinson with the train awaiting orders. The next day we were ordered to this place where we found the regiment. Four companies have since

been ordered to London. The rest are encamped at this place.

There was considerable excitement here last Friday night on hearing the rebels had burned a train at Crab Orchard, a distance of eight miles from here. I am informed by an eye witness that after burning the train they went into town and were welcomed by the ladies of the place who were dressed in white, each one bearing a rebel design. After congratulations and other preliminaries, they were feasted on the choicest luxuries of the season which the citizens had been preparing for them for several days.

Some of the rebel ladies had also told my informant that the rebels were coming in on that night several days previous to the time. After spending half the night in their revelry, they left but we succeeded in capturing 41 out of 44 of them.

The train consisted of 27 wagons and was loaded with ammunition, clothing, etc. The men were mostly citizens of the place who had enlisted under Morgan. John W. Graham of our company was captured while bearing a dispatch from Danville to Lebanon last week by three of Morgan's men who had succeeded in penetrating our lines. They took his dispatch, money, his mother's miniature and his boots, broke his gun and let him go as they hadn't time to parole him.

You say you have some notion of enlisting in the state guards. If I understand the duty of a state guard, you would be obliged to go into camp as prisoner guards or to defend the state. If you leave home and go in camp, it would be far more satisfactory and honorable to go into the field. The home guard, or d--d militia as they are called by most, are looked on with contempt by soldiers in the field. It is not my wish to influence you in the choice of service, but merely give my opinion.

In regard to going home, I am sorry to say my hopes are blasted again. The issuing of furloughs is left to the discretion of commanders of departments. General Wilcox has been relieved by General Hartsuf in command of our department, and one of the first things General Hartsuf done on taking command was to veto all furloughs. I may not get to go home now until I am discharged, but I shall bear with my fate whatever it may be as a true soldier should. Discontent is the cause of a great proportion of the sickness in camp, but I have never allowed it to affect me in the least. I take everything as it comes and am satisfied.

Camp Dick Robinson, Kentucky
August 7, 1863

You have heard of the recent raid in this state and are anxious to hear of the part taken in it by the 44th. The first move that was made was this: five of the six companies stationed at Stanford were ordered to Mount Vernon, there to await orders. I obtained permission from the Q.M. and went along in hopes of seeing a little of the elephant.

On arriving at Mount Vernon, we heard that the four companies at London were fighting with the rebs and were ordered to meet them halfway at Wild Cat and make a stand. I thought this looked like work and if I wanted to see any of the fun I had better get a gun, which I succeeded in doing after going nearly all over the regiment. On arriving at Wild Cat, I heard that companies A, C and G (London detachment) had been skirmishing with the rebel advance for nearly one and a half days, holding them back at every favorable position until they by the advantage of superior numbers would flank them when they would have to give way to the next favorable position. On hearing that Company G was only seven miles out, I started out but found them after going three miles, they having been relieved by another company. The rebs declined fighting us at Wild Cat and went around us in the direction of Richmond. We were then ordered back to Hickman's bridge but left our camp behind and started out the next day. Were out about two weeks and returned to this place. They had several unimportant skirmishes but met with no losses except two prisoners at London where the three companies of our regiment killed two and wounded four.

*The regiment is laboring under a great excitement now occasioned by an order that we should be dismounted. The excitement ran so high last evening that the Lt. Col. capped his navies and went out among them swearing the noise must be stopped. Such expressions were heard as "we'll desert," "Hurrah for the 44th" and "death to Col. Gilbert" (the officer who had us dismounted), etc. We may expect trouble as the 44th is made up of a set of hot-blooded men who will **fight**, but to anger them is like stirring up a volcano. They **must** have vent to their feelings regardless of cost.*

August 8th. We are turning over horses and equipment today and will be paid off in a few days. Several furloughs

Union forces under Major General Ambrose E. Burnside marching into eastern Tennessee, August 1863

were received this week that were forwarded on the 15th of May. Kent has received one and will start for home soon as we are paid off. There is still some hopes of getting mine.

Why not send those miniatures you spoke of by mail. I would receive them very gladly. It is unnecessary to send papers as we receive them the day they are printed. We have just received news of Scipio Myer's nomination for Representative. It meets with universal approbation. I believe I get a vote this fall, don't I? Examine and let me know as I want to be sure.

By mid-August 1863, the invasion of east Tennessee got underway. Union forces under General Burnside totaled 24,000 men and outnumbered the Confederate defenders by four to one. Burnside bypassed the Confederate stronghold at Cumberland Gap and marched directly to Knoxville, meeting with little resistance from the Confederates who abandoned the city in late August. Turning their attention to Cumberland Gap, the Union army forced the surrender of that place on September 10. Because of the strong Union sympathy that prevailed in eastern Tennessee, its "liberation" had long been awaited, not only by the government but many of the citizens of that area. Militarily, the occupation of eastern Tennessee deprived the Confederates of direct rail transportation between Chattanooga and the East.

Knoxville, Tennessee
September 15, 1863
In coming back from the Gap, we intended to march to the nearest station and ride the rest of the way on the cars. A train was sent for the purpose, guarded by 250 of the 100th Ohio, part of our brigade, but they were met with about five times their number of Rebs and were all taken prisoners after a hard fight in which they killed more than their number and had six of their own men killed. The train, however, got back safe.

Without being here and hearing it from the citizens, one can hardly form an idea of the Union sentiment among the people or the way they have been treated by the rebels. While marching through the state to this place, the people almost went crazy with joy.

While riding in front of the column one day, a woman

A soldier, convicted of horse-stealing, is drummed through the town.

with two good looking daughters came out saying,, "You are strangers but you are the first Union soldiers I have ever seen and we must shake hands with you." Another lady where I stopped to get dinner says, "I am not a wicked woman, was raised by good old Presbyterian parents but I have swore a stack of oaths as high as the heavens and I don't think I will be held accountable for it." Her child's name was George and she said she dared not call it by its name in presence of the Rebs for fear of being insulted for naming him of General George B. McClellan. At another place, a man nearly 100 years old stood at the gate with water for us while his wife carried it from the spring. Some places we would see a Union man stripped of everything while his neighbor, a rebel, had plenty of everything.

We had an exciting time this afternoon. The division was called out under arms, taken to town and placed on each side of the streets when a Kentucky soldier who had stolen a horse and mule was drummed through the town with a card fastened to his breast on which was printed in large letters the word "Thief." One side of his head was shaved and the letter "T" was branded on his left cheek. He is to work on some public works the rest of his enlistment. This is the penalty for stealing, according to an order issued by General Burnside on coming into the state.

I suppose you are anxious to hear a description of Cumberland Gap. I am incapable to give anything like a good description of the place, but I will do the best I can. When viewed from this side at a distance of three miles, it looks like an immense gap between two ridges of mountains, the peaks of which are one mile apart. On arriving at the foot of the mountain you see on your right a ridge of rocks nearly perpendicular and almost one mile high. On your left, the mountain is not quite so steep nor as high but presents the same scraggy, rocky appearance. In front you see a crooked road winding along the side of each mountain and up the ravine between them. On the road, owing to its being so crooked, it is one mile from the base of the mountain to the top of the gap. On going to the top of the peak on your right you can see a distance of 35 miles in almost any direction. It is a grand sight to see the valleys, rivers, mountains and farms from a position like this. After viewing the scenery, *you can step back a few yards and by walking around a large cornerstone you can say you have been in three states, viz., Kentucky, Virginia and Tennessee. In descending on the other side, it is not so steep but resembles the other side in many respects.*

The rebels had all these places strongly fortified, making it one of the strongest places in the United States. The only way to take it by force would be to shell them off part of the mountain at a time by day and take possession by night with infantry protecting them with breastworks. And this could only be done with considerable loss.

I have not seen a paper for a long time. If you have any that contain accounts of our operations or anything else of interest, I would be very thankful for them. The last news we have is up to the 5th. Also, can you get me a pair of boots made and send them by Jack Martin or John Olwine. I want size five, kip, double sole, stiff counter, high tops and a heel that won't run down. Such a boot would cost here 10 or 12 dollars. If you can get them made and sent down with price, I will send you the money. Let me know in your next.

In the meantime, Union forces in middle Tennessee under Major General William S. Rosecrans initiated an offensive which culminated in the battle of Chickamauga and a bloody defeat of Rosecrans' army. With the Federal forces bottled up in Chattanooga, Major General Braxton Bragg ill advisedly weakened his besieging army by sending Lt. General James Longstreet with 15,000 men to drive Burnside's forces out of Knoxville.

Provost Marshal's Office
Knoxville, Tennessee
December 5, 1863

We are at last relieved of a siege of 21 days this morning and I will improve the earliest opportunity of writing you a few lines. The Rebs under Longstreet attacked our outposts on the 14th and on the 16th had us cooped up except on the opposite side of the river. There is one road which they never had possession of, although they captured several forage wagons, two of which were from our regiment. They took three men with the wagons.

There was some confusion here when we heard that our

Defending against Longstreet's assault on Fort Sanders

The Yankees recover a hog caught between the lines.

outposts were being driven in and some of the timid commenced making preparations for a retreat. But when General Burnside arrived here on the 16th, he issued an order in which he said, "There has not nor will there be any arrangements made looking to a retreat." He says, "We will stay right here and fight it out one way or the other." He also began making active preparations for a defense. Fortifications were built encircling the town, except one side of town where about 100 houses including depot station houses and arsenal were. Most of these houses were subsequently burned to prevent them from being infested by rebel sharpshooters.

Everything was put in shape to stand a siege. Rations were reduced one half and as flour began to get scarce our bread was made of shorts. Toward the end of the siege it was reduced to nearly pure bran. I wish I could send you a loaf of siege bread — it would be a curiosity.

On the sixth day of the siege, our brigade was called upon to charge the rifle pits of the skirmishers, which they done in fine style. They drove the skirmishers back to their reserve and burned a house which had been infested by their sharpshooters. General Sanders was killed the same day. He was a brave as well as a good general. Our brigade which had up to this time been held in reserve was ordered across the river, after which it stood on the skirmish line every third day.

Our regiment had several amusing incidents while skirmishing. At one time the Rebs got after a hog, and in trying to kill it drove it outside their lines when our boys shot it. As it was between the lines, the only way they could get it was to show the Rebs a Yankee trick which they done by reenforcing the line from the reserve and directing such a fire on the rebel pits that it was dangerous for one to show his head while one went out and drug the hog in. Two of our men made an agreement the same day with two Rebs, laid down their arms and had a chat together.

On the 29th, the Rebs' four brigades made a charge on Fort Sanders which proved an entire failure. Their loss was about 1,000 while we lost only nine. They came so close under the fort that the artillerymen lit the fuse of shells with cigars and tossed them by hand into a ditch where they bursted, killing a great many. I went out to the scene of action after the fight. It was the most horrible sight I ever saw. In the ditch the men lay in some places three deep in every position, doubled up just as they had rolled down the embankment.

After the fight there was a cessation of hostilities until 5 p.m. when the Rebs and our men came out of their trenches and had a long talk together. All along the line could be seen squads of Rebs and Yanks talking and joking as though they were the best friends imaginable. But at 5 p.m. every man was in his place just as anxious to take each others' lives as ever.

It has been over two months since I heard from you, but I hope I will get two or three letters soon as communications are open. Deserters are coming in rapidly this morning. The streets are full of them. They report that Longstreet's army is completely demoralized and would nearly all desert if they had chances.

Our 1st Lieutenant, Thompson, was wounded slightly in the back with a shell. We had one killed in the regiment and four or five wounded. During the siege the Rebs threw several shells in town but did little damage.

Camp Nelson, Kentucky
December 29, 1863

No doubt you are surprised to see my letter dated at this place. The Tennessee brigade started from Knoxville, December 14th and arrived here on the 17th, and I along with them as brigade commissary clerk. We brought with us 523 rebel prisoners mostly captured during the siege of Knoxville. We had a very nice trip of it and good weather for the time of the year.

Our brigade consists of the 8th, 9th, 16th and 17th East Tennessee Cav. and are all new regiments. They are sent here to be recruited, organized and drilled, which will take probably two months or more. The brigade numbers about seven hundred men for duty at the present time. The brigade is commanded by Colonel Casement of the 103rd Ohio. His staff is from the 103rd and 104th O.V.I. Three officers of the 104th were ordered back to their regiments soon as they arrived here so that I am the only one of our brigade remaining with this brigade. The commissary that I am *clerking for belongs to the 103rd O.V.I. and was not ordered to his regiment.*

The day before leaving Knoxville, I received 4 letters from home. I received miniatures of mother and yourself for which you will please receive my sincere thanks. The miniatures are very good.

Can you or Father come down to see me? I suppose it would be impossible for me to get a leave of absence.

In the fall of 1863 plans were developed for the reorganization of the 44th Ohio into a cavalry unit. Major Alpheus S. Moore, who had been promoted earlier that year from command of Company A, wrote the following letter to general Burnside:

"Head Qrs. 44th Ohio Vols.
Knoxville, Nov. 14th, 1863

"General!

I have the honor to submit to your judgment the following plan for the organization of a Cav. Regt.

"I wish to get authority to recruit from the old three years' regiments now in the field, especially from the 44th Ohio Vol. Infty. under the late orders for reenlisting veteran volunteers. A large portion of the 44th Ohio, both officers and men will reenter the service with me on this plan, but they will never reenlist as Infty.

"I propose that the officers and men enrolled as above mentioned shall form the skeleton of a complete cavalry regt. to be filled up with recruits from Ohio and to be officered entirely by men of two or more years' experience in the field.

"I propose to conduct the recruiting in the following manner:

"Having secured from the governor of Ohio authority to raise a cavalry regiment, I desire to take the officers and men enlisted here, north in a body to some convenient rendezvous and there organize them into recruiting parties thereby using them to complete the new organization and at the same time giving them the thirty days' furlough allowed by law to veteran volunteers who reenlist, and without which very few will reenter the service.

"The advantages of this scheme are in my opinion as follows:

"1st — It will secure to the government the service of a large number of 1st class soldiers who otherwise will not reenlist.

"2nd — It will form a command officered entirely by men of experience with in Infty. and Mtd. service.

"3rd — The presence and influence of experienced and well disciplined soldiers in such numbers will give tone to the whole body and secure an efficiency which cannot otherwise be obtained except by long service and hard labor.

"Hoping that the above will meet the approbation of the Gen'l Comdg. I am Sir

> With Much Respect
> Yours to Command
> A.S. Moore
> Maj. 44th Ohio"

The matter of reenlistment and reorganization was worked out over the next few weeks. On December 30th Colonel Gilbert wrote to General Potter, then serving as Chief of Staff for the Department of Ohio. His letter is as follows:

"I have the honor to ask for answers to the following questions which have been raised by officers and men in reference to their reenlistment as veteran volunteers.

"1st — In case three fourths of the regt. reenlist will the furlough of 30 days promised in the orders be given them within twenty days if there is no immediate prospect of a battle?

"2d — When and where will the bounty due on their discharge from their present term of enlistment, and the advanced pay and bounty be paid?

"3rd — Will you give the furlough to companies or individuals that reenlist if the regiment fails to go in as a whole, on the same terms and time as promised to the regiment?

"4th — What will be done with field staff and line officers who may decline to go in if the whole regiment reenlists?

"5th — Can men now members of the regiment be reenlisted as veterans in other arms of the service?

"6th — Can you give any assurances in case the regiment reenlists under your promise of having them mounted that that promise would be respected by your successors in case you should not remain in command of this Department?

"7th — In case the **whole** regiment does not reenlist under your promise to have them mounted would all be mounted or only those who reenlist?

"As the time in which to reenlist veterans is short and many of the officers and men will delay reenlisting until the above questions are answered. I have the honor to ask for your speedy consideration of them.

"With much respect

> Your Obdt. Servt.
> S.A. Gilbert
> Col. 44th Regt. O.V.I."

1864

"James, there is some men that never saw the elephant, but I have saw him. I have saw his head and tail."

Pvt. John Barrack
Co. G., 8th Ohio Vol. Cav.
August 14, 1864

1864

ON THE 1st OF JANUARY, the proposal to reenlist was made to the men of the regiment, accompanied by the promise that they should be armed and mounted as a cavalry unit. Apparently the questions raised by Colonel Gilbert had been answered to the satisfaction of most of the men, for over 90 percent of the regiment reenlisted on January 5th. On the 7th they marched for Camp Nelson, Kentucky.[1]

Colonel Gilbert was in Ohio ahead of the regiment and working on plans for reorganization. At the state capitol, Columbus, he advised the state adjutant general's office of his plans:

"I have the honor to inform you that the 44th Regt. O.V.I. has reenlisted as veteran Vols. and is now on its way home under orders from Maj. Gen. Foster, Comdg. Dept. of the Ohio copies of which please find enclosed by which you will see that Battery D 1st O.V.A. which also reenlisted is with my command.

"They will reach Camp Nelson, Kentucky, tomorrow and will be then mustered and paid. I reported to Governor Brough this morning and was directed by him to you for orders as to the point to which I shall take them from which to send them on furlough as per orders of War Dept. In this connection I will respectfully suggest Springfield, Clark Co. that being the place where the 44th Reg. originally assembled and is central and convenient to the homes of the men."[2]

On January 8, 1864, Maj. General Foster, commander of the Department of the Ohio, issued the following order:

"By the Direction of Sec'y of War the 44th Ohio Vol. Infty. will be reorganized as a veteran cavalry regiment and the C.O. will take such steps as are necessary to complete the organization. It will proceed at once to Camp Nelson, Kentucky, and there turn over the infantry arms and equipments thence proceeding as already ordered."[3]

The order was directed to the commanding officer of the regiment.

It was the end of the month before the furloughed regiment reached Springfield after overcoming a great amount of red tape in connection with the reorganization and the journey home. Until the last the train had been scheduled to go to Columbus instead of Springfield but through Colonel Gilbert's insistence it was permitted to alter its course.

The citizens of Springfield and the surrounding area were ready for them. They had been preparing for the homecoming for days and had kept in touch with the progress of the furlough train. Upon reaching Springfield, the soldiers were greeted by a huge throng and were given a hero's welcome. The Lewisburg cannon heralded their arrival to the city. There was a parade, a huge feast, and a speech by Samuel Shellabarger. Banners read "Welcome Our Brave," and "Lewisburg was the neatest little stand-up fight of the war — Rosecrans."

Colonel Gilbert was called upon to address the crowd, and before concluding his remarks, he led the men of the regiment in a resounding three cheers as an expression of their gratitude for the support of the community. He also admonished his men as follows: "My lads, it only remains for me to remind you that strict discipline is as necessary while you are home among your friends, as it is in the field." The men were paid off and given a 30-day furlough.

The local newspaper devoted a full page to the celebration and listed the names of the men who reenlisted and those who had not. It also carried a poem dedicated to the 44th, the last stanza of which read:

> "Then let the cannon loudly roar
> A welcome to their homes once more,
> The heroes of the Forty-Fourth,
> These hardy veterans of the North,
> Who long have fought on the battle plain
> And ready are to fight again." [4]

On March 14, 1864, Colonel Gilbert was constrained to issue the following circular regarding alleged misconduct of his men while on furlough:

"The attention of officers and soldiers is called to complaints made to the Governor of the State, of the lawless conduct of soldiers said to belong to this regiment. Some of these are, no doubt, groundless, or in the main chargeable to evil-disposed citizens, dressed as soldiers, or to members of other regiments.

"Wherever you have heretofore served, your reputation for good discipline and soldierly conduct has been so thoroughly established that no one ever before thought of bringing such charges against you.

"I trust all members of the Regiment will see to it that this good reputation, won by hard service in the field, is not lost through the folly of a few thoughtless men countenancing these mischievous excesses, or by the negligence of some careless officer, who thus demonstrates his unfitness for command.

"Your mission in this contest is to meet the armed rebels in the field, and by conquering them, restore the rightful authority of the Government over states in open rebellion. You have nothing to do with the miserable faction here, who so far forget their manhood as to be willing to submit to the dismemberment of our country, without an effort to save it from the destruction and disgrace that would be entailed by the success of those with whom they sympathize.

"Here the civil authorities are in full power, and we can safely leave in their hands the punishment of any treasonable acts committed by the secret enemies of the Republic in our midst. You must not be guilty of unlawful acts on their account, thus gratifying their absurd charges of usurpation of power, by which they endeavor to excite the people against the Government and against the army.

"It is the duty of all officers, at all times, to interfere to prevent soldiers, whether of their own command or not, from committing any breach of the peace, or otherwise doing anything that will bring the army into disrepute, and any who fail in this will be guilty of gross negligence of duty.

"Any officer or soldier of this regiment who is charged with any offense against the law will be promptly arrested and turned over to the civil authorities for trial." [5]

Camp Dennison, Ohio
April 2, 1864
We arrived here yesterday evening at 8:30 p.m. We were about a half hour finding our quarters and were soon enjoying the soft side of a board much to the discomfort of the recruits who were grumbling all night, thereby disturbing the otherwise quiet sleep of the veterans. It seems quite natural to come down to the usual sowbelly and hardtack after feasting on the

luxuries of home. No doubt we will look back upon the fleshpots of Darke County with wishful eyes and wish that the Southern Confederacy could be whipped out as well by staying at home on furlough as to go into camp.

The men are all in excellent spirits today and not any of them under the influence of spirits. They have caught a rabbit that was attempting to cross the river and have been amusing themselves by forming a large ring and letting the rabbit loose on the inside and then recapturing it.

I suppose you have heard of the accident which occurred with one of our men the evening before we left. We came very near coming in contact with the police of Dayton. They accused one of our company of stealing a hat at one of the stores of that place. He proved that he had paid for the hat and the company also offered to pay for it, but the police (five or six in number) said it was not the hat but the man they wanted and lay hold on him when he was rescued by the company amidst the cheers of a large crowd who were looking on.

At Xenia some of the home guards attempted to arrest one of our men for getting into a quarrel with the proprietor of a restaurant. Although the soldier was in the wrong, he was protected by the company who were not willing that a veteran should be arrested by a state guard. They afterward settled the dispute satisfactorily with the proprietor.

We will draw clothing this afternoon but have no idea how soon we will be mounted or draw our arms or how long we will stay here. The company from Dayton and also the one from Yellow Springs went home this morning to vote. Our company was not allowed to go on account of the distance and having just arrived.

We have good quarters. The mud is very slippery but not deep.

Camp Dennison, Ohio
April 14, 1864

We are getting along well. Have heard nothing of our horses yet. Expect to stay here two or three weeks yet.

We are very busy making our muster rolls which is my apology for a short letter.

Camp Dennison, Ohio
April 22, 1864

We are still here and with no more reliable prospect of leaving than at the date of my last. We have drawn a few sabres with which the noncommissioned officers are drilled two hours each day. If business and activity are antidotes for the blues, I think that any fears on my part of that fearful malady would be entirely unnecessary. The first week after arriving at camp, I was busily engaged in the Q.M. department as clerk and only returned to the company to find two or three more weeks' hard work on hand at making out muster rolls. In addition to that, by virtue of having been appointed Q.M. Sergeant, am required to digest five pages of Cooks Cavalry Tactics and recite every other night. So you see that between writing, studying and reciting, I have hardly time to eat let alone getting homesick. There, I have used the phrase Q.M. Sergeant and have not complied with your request to explain it. So here goes. My position is Quartermaster Sergeant of the company and my consequent duties are to draw and issue clothing, keep the clothing book, draw and issue horses' equipment, arms, etc., and also to attend to them when on march. I get one dollar per month more than a duty sergeant, have no picket or guard duty to perform or any drilling to do unless I do it voluntarily.

I am drilling and studying the sabre exercise, have got through studying it and only want a little more practice to attain a considerable degree of perfection in it. I can go through all the movements, but it requires practice to go through them with precision and dexterity.

A company of cavalry — there, I have used the word company when there is no such word as company in cavalry. It should be squadron. But who wouldn't make mistakes? I am writing in the captain's quarters (a room 10 feet square) and there are — well, I won't take the time to count them, but there are at least 15 persons in the room and they are all jabbering away like so many monkeys. What a comparison — a soldier compared to a monkey! But what was I going to say? O, yes, a squadron of cavalry (right this time) is composed of one captain, two lieutenants, one first sergeant, one Q.M. sergeant, one commissary sergeant and five duty sergeants.

April 23. I was obliged to lay my letter to one side last evening and make out a muster roll for the recruits. It took until 2 a.m. They will probably be paid off today. The vets will not be paid off for a month or so yet. The question as to whether we will be mounted here is at last settled. We received 17 carloads of horses (250) this morning and are to receive 300 more tomorrow. I think the indications are now that we will leave about the last of next week.

Shields and Jarvis have not had their trial yet but the penalty in such cases, with about 20 that have been tried, is one month's wages and wages during the time of absence taken from them besides an introduction and a berth in the guardhouse for a week or two.

I received the money you sent me ($10.00) and am very grateful for it. If I had known the recruits would have been paid off so soon, I would have borrowed from them and not asked it of you. Have my photos been finished yet? If so, send me two in your next.

If you have a copy of any paper containing an account of the Butternut skirmish in Greenville, please cut it out and send it to me. If not, give as good an account of it as you can if it is not too much trouble.

Tell the children they must all go to school and learn fast.

My outfit will cost about $30. I got a Macintosh and four saddle bags yesterday that cost $23. The company are all getting them. We will be well equipped. A Macintosh is a green overcoat, coated over with something like felt like a hat. It is used to either turn rain or cold.

There are over 60 men in guardhouse for absence without leave, none from our company.

Camp Dennison, Ohio
April 29, 1864

We started for Kanawha Valley this p.m. Direct here. No more. We leave in five minutes. Only six companies go. We have no horses. The other six companies stay and are mounted.

Charleston, Western Virginia
May 4, 1864

I dropped you a line at Camp Dennison on the 1st in which I stated that we were on the eve of starting for this place. We went to Cincinnati that evening, lay there overnight and took a steamer the next morning for this place where we arrived yesterday at 2 p.m.

There has been a forward movement from this place of about 30,000 men, and six companies of our regiment were ordered to come here to act as guards to protect communications while the other six companies are to remain at Camp D to draw horses and equipment for the whole regiment when they will join us at this place. But I suppose you think we would make a poor out at protecting communications without arms? So we would, but we have drawn infantry arms for a portion of the command while the rest would take clubs or stones. No doubt we would make a strong fight.

There were about a dozen guerrillas captured within a few miles of here last week. The 34th Ohio left here with the column last week. Sam'l Paliner and Wm. George and James Hamilton are here yet, not having been able to march with the command. They are not seriously ill but are able to leave their quarters.

The Kanawha Valley presents the same desolate appearance that it did when we left. The streets of Charleston, owing to the large number of troops who have been here lately and the amount of rain, are about three feet deep with mud, although we have good quarters and are not troubled with mud. We went into quarters which had been built by the 23rd Ohio Inf. and occupied by them for 12 months.

I suppose the national guards have taken the field ere this. I would like to see some of them on a march. While coming up on the boat, as we were passing Boontown, a number of kid glove gents came to the wharf and began waving their handkerchiefs when the men commenced hollering, "How are you conscripts?" "Malish," etc. Of course, handkerchiefs were soon pocketed and gents began making themselves scarce.

Charleston, West Virginia
May 13, 1864

I sent you Col. Gilbert's reason for resigning. The second battalion joined us from Camp D. today. Will remain here some time. Have not heard from you since leaving Camp D. I wrote to you soon after arriving here.

Think matters look to a termination of the war this summer, don't you?

**Samuel A. Gilbert, Colonel,
8th Ohio Cavalry Breveted Brigadier General**

Courtesy of Massachusetts Commandery, Military Order of the Loyal Legion
and the U.S. Army Military History Institute

Shaw is major. McAlpine is Capt., Co. G. Creeger, having been reduced to ranks by Col. Gilbert, is a private. In reference to that, mum is the word. Moore is Col. of the regiment, not Frank Moore, but A.S. Moore, formerly major. Col. Gilbert's loss is deeply felt in the regiment although Moore makes an excellent cavalry officer.

Charleston, West Virginia
May 16, 1864

The other six companies joined us from Camp Dennison two days ago bringing with them horses for the rest of the command so that we are now mounted but not armed, except with the infantry arms we drawed shortly after our arrival. Each company in the regiment has drawn horses of a different color. Our squadron has browns: Company B has sorrels; one company has all blacks, etc. We have only a tolerable lot of horses. There are a great many poor ones among them.

It will take two or three weeks to arm and equip the command and shoe the horses, but parts of the regiment may be supplied and ordered to the front first.

I sent you one of Col. Gilbert's pamphlets in which he gives reasons for resigning and also comes down pretty heavy on some of Governor Brough's actions concerning our regiment. Suppose you have read it and are prepared by this time to give your opinion concerning it. I think Gov. Brough has greatly injured the efficiency of our regiment in promoting the men according to rank instead of according to the election held by the men. Besides, as long as he persists in that course there is no incentive to exertion. A noncommissioned officer may be ever so indolent and careless, yet if he can avoid being reduced to the ranks he stands as good a chance for promotion as those who are the most diligent — but enough of this.

Colonel Gilbert's pamphlet, published at Camp Dennison, Ohio, on April 25, 1864, commenced by stating that it was his duty to publish the following extract from General Orders, No. 153, War Department, Adjutant General's Office: "Col. S.A. Gilbert, 44th Ohio Volunteers, having tendered his resignation, is hereby honorably discharged the service of the United States on account of physical disability." The order was dated April 20, 1864. Colonel Gilbert stated that his health was not the only reason which "impelled" him to tender his resignation. When the officers and men of the 44th reenlisted, they had been assured by Colonel Gilbert that all vacancies in commissions in the new regiment would be filled by election, but when Colonel Gilbert forwarded the recommendations from the regiment, they were ignored by Governor Brough who made his own choices. This caused a great embarrassment to Colonel Gilbert who resigned.

The pamphlet also included a copy of the petition signed by all of the commissioned officers requesting the War Department to refuse the resignation. The petition carried the same date as the War Department's acceptance and was not received in time to be considered before the order was entered.[6]

Correspondent Zouave would write from Camp Dennison on April 23, 1864, regarding Colonel Gilbert's resignation:

"The regiment unanimously protested against the acceptance of the resignation. Nevertheless it was accepted. Ohio has lost her best Colonel — the cause one of its staunchest and most earnest defenders. The soul of the 44th has left it, and there is no man in it but will mourn the loss. — Everything the regiment has done is identified with Colonel Gilbert. His influences pervaded every element in it. Its victories were the consummation of his plans. He trained them as carefully as a father trains his child, and shared all its dangers and hardships. Not a man is in it but is willing to face death and fall at his bidding. With it he has turned defeat into victory, and converted disaster into success. Wherever he goes the esteem of the regiment accompany him." [7]

While the state of his health was the legal reason for his resignation, it is obvious that Colonel Gilbert's principal reason was his great dissatisfaction with the appointments by Governor Brough. For the next two months the *Springfield Republic* carried letters by him setting forth his reasons for resigning and accusing the Governor of bad faith in the matter. Articles also contained letters from the administration questioning whether it would even be appropriate to reappoint Colonel Gilbert when he had been found physically unfit for military duty; the administration's policy regarding the change in procedures for selecting officers was also defended.

Colonel Gilbert, who had been in poor health since the Knoxville campaign, was breveted brigadier general on March 13, 1865. He died on June 9, 1868, at age 40. Governor Brough's health also failed, and he died in office on August 29, 1865.

Colonel Gilbert was a native of Zanesville where his father,

Charles Champion Gilbert, had been its first Mayor. The colonel's son, Cass Gilbert, born in 1859, became a world-famous architect whose notable works included the Woolworth Building in New York, the United States Supreme Court building, several state capitol buildings, many public buildings and, ironically enough, the state capitol building of West Virginia at Charleston, the city his father had helped to defend many years before when his son was but a few years old.

> *In the clipping from some paper which you sent me, I find the 44th has credit for a share in the glory of the Butternut fight in Greenville although there was not a man of us there. I suppose they knew our hearts were in the cause and deemed it as bad to think as to do, but I suppose it is getting pretty quiet there now as I have not heard of any late demonstrations.*

In *The Crisis,* an anti-administration newspaper in Columbus, the following article appeared on April 27, 1864:

"Desperate Outrages of Soldiers in Darke County — We learn that the returned soldiers at Greenville, Darke County, on last week, took possession of that town, beat several Democrats dangerously, shot one so that his life was despaired of, riddled the Hon. Wm. Allen's law office with bullets, and then broke up the furniture; did much other damage, and finally compelled the Democrats to close their places of business, their residences, etc., and fly for safety. The home Republicans cheering on the work of destruction. Would it not be well for Gov. Brough to proclaim martial law in Darke County?" [8]

John McKee's assessment that the men of the 44th were not involved in any misconduct occurring in April was probably correct since they were back in camp by then and no longer on furlough.

> *I believe I never saw worse weather than we have had since we came here. We landed in a drenching rain, and it has rained almost incessantly ever since. I am writing in a log shanty, 10x15, covered with shelter tents. The rain has begun to increase in vigor since I commenced this letter. As the thin shelter tents are a very poor protection from the rain, I fear I will be obliged to give this letter up ere it is finished. I think it altogether probable that things will go swimmingly here soon if the clouds keep up their constant supply of rain much longer.*

I think it is a mistake about Isaac Keefauver having been drowned. I see some of his company almost every day, yet none of them have mentioned anything about it. There was however a man drowned at Soop Creek, 35 miles above here, from that regiment. It may be possible it was him, but I think it not probable.

The war news are very cheering. I can't see how the Rebs are going to hold out much longer at this rate. There is one thing certain. The public mind has become in earnest and demands a termination of this war this summer.

Meadow Bluffs, West Virginia
June 2, 1864

We arrived here this evening. Are ordered to send everything back to Charleston except one change of clothing. Was even ordered to send back my photo album, but expect to smuggle it along. We leave tomorrow to join Generals Averell and Crook who left here yesterday. Are told we will be out about one month.

It is the prevailing opinion that we will go to East Virginia and remain there if Grant is successful.

Staunton, Virginia
June 8, 1864

I have 15 minutes to write you by a campfire and send by three regiments that go home tomorrow. Have made a raid here where we joined General Hunter, are destroying railroads, etc. Will probably start for Gordonsville or some other place in two or three days. Hunter had a sharp engagement 12 miles from here at Port Republic in which he completely routed Rebs who fled to mountains. We have come 210 miles and are now on the extreme right of the Army of the Potomac.

— The regiments have not left yet, so I will write a little more. We had one day's rations issued to us this morning which is all we are to get until we return to some line of communications. There is a diversity of opinion as to where that will be, but it will not be the Kanawha. We will be obliged to forage off the country. We had an easy march here, not more than 20 miles per day. Seen no fighting except bushwhacking. One man in our regiment wounded in arm, three killed out of other regiments.

Gauley, West Virginia
June 30, 1864

After a long and perilous march of nearly 700 miles during which we endured hardships unprecedented in my experience as a soldier, I am happy to announce to you that I with my usual good fortune have arrived at the haven of rest although we have left several of our brave men in rebel hands.

On arriving at Lewisburg, we were thrown in a brigade of General Averell's division. The next day, we started in direction of Staunton with three brigades of cavalry and three brigades of infantry under command of General Crook. On arriving there, we found it in possession of General Hunter who had occupied it after a severe fight at Piedmont, 12 miles distant. They were engaged in destroying rebel property. Railroad, machinery, factories and bridges shared one common ruin.

Staunton is a place of considerable importance to the Rebs. It is larger than Greenville, is situated in a beautiful as well as very fertile valley, contains a number of rebel factories and other buildings of great importance to them.

After leaving this place, two days' march brought us to Lexington where we halted one day to draw rations and clothing which had been sent to us from Martinsburg in a train of 200 wagons. You can hardly imagine my surprise at 10 a.m. of the day we were here when cousin McHorner pulled me out of my tent with the salutation "Hallo, John, wake up! How are you." Capt. Orr then came up with "Come, come, old fellow. What does this mean." I was totally at a loss how to account for their presence there at that time, but an explanation proved that they had come through as guards for the train. I then procured a pass and went three miles to where their regiment was encamped where I saw Uncle Naylor and all the company in fine spirits and anxious to accompany us to Lynchburg, but this was denied them. They, however, accompanied us to the foot of the Blue Ridge where we crossed the James River. Here the last of the rations were issued to us and the last that we received until two days ago when near this place. This was the last we saw of the 152nd. How far they accompanied us or when and where they went, I am not able to say.

The second morning after leaving Staunton, we left a man suspended between Heaven and earth by a stout hempen

Hunter's Lynchburg Raiders

neckerchief with a card on his breast containing the words, "Murderer of a Union Soldier." His negroes informed on him and he acknowledged the crime. Several others were shot at different times for bushwhacking us along the road which was carried on to a considerable extent, killing a number out of other regiments and seriously wounding one of our regiment.

The man executed by the Union forces was David S. Creigh, who lived in Greenbrier County near Lewisburg, West Virginia. In his report on the Lynchburg campaign, Brig. Gen. William W. Averell, commanding the Second Cavalry Division of Hunter's army, stated that "On the 2d Mr. David Creigh, a citizen of Lewisburg, was tried by a military commission and found guilty of murdering a Union soldier in November last. The proceedings were subsequently approved, and Mr. Creigh was hanged at Belleview on Friday, the 10th of June." [9] On November 8, 1862, Mr. Creigh, upon arriving home to find the soldier pillaging the house and being abusive to the women in the home, killed the Union soldier in an altercation with him. With the aid of a slave the body was buried. When the Union forces returned to Lewisburg the following May, word was received about the incident, and upon the finding of the soldier's body, Mr. Creigh was arrested, tried by military commission without benefit of counsel, convicted and sentenced to death. He accompanied the army to Staunton pending confirmation of the proceedings and sentence by Major General David Hunter, Department Commander. Following his execution and burial at Belleview, his body was recovered by his family and buried in Lewisburg. He had been a well-known and respected citizen of that community and is referred to as the Greenbrier martyr.[10]

At Lexington, we burned Governor Letcher's residence after giving his wife 10 minutes to remove valuable property. We also burned a state military institute which had just been vacated by 300 students.

On arriving near Lynchburg, our regiment was sent out as skirmishers. We drove the rebel skirmishers behind their entrenchments when we were driven back by a brigade of Rebs. But the Rebs unexpectedly ran against a division under General Crook which sent them pell mell back to their entrenchments. It was now getting dark, and our regiment was sent 1/2 mile to the rear to graze our horses (as we had no other feed during the whole raid) and the day's work was ended by a few tunes from a band such as "We'll Rally Around the Flag, Boys," etc. — for the benefit of the Rebs, of course.

The next morning, we mounted and took position about 300 yards in rear and in plain view of our lines. We were in range of their artillery, several shots lighting in our midst wounding two men. At about 10 a.m., the Rebs massed their forces and tried to break the line in front of where our regiment was stationed, but our line was quickly reinforced from the reserve, and they were hurled back with considerable loss. They tried it the second and third time, but our veterans were invincible. Each assault was as unsuccessful as the first. The three charges were made in about two hours during which time we remained at the same place viewing the terrible conflict — in range of shells but not allowed to take part. Our duty was to protect the rear in case our line was repulsed.

I wish I could give you even a fair description of the battle, but that is impossible. The scene can only be realized by those who have been eye witnesses of similar incidents. During each charge, only the outlines of regiments and brigades could be seen through the smoke and dense column of dust, hurrying to a weak place in the line or charging like fiends incarnate on the rebel lines until they drove them behind their strong entrenchments when they would fall back to their position. Canister, grape and shell were freely used, filling the air with their deafening sounds. In the evening, we were again sent to the rear to graze.

At about 9 p.m., we were ordered out and soon found that our army had all started on a retreat and that our brigade was detailed as rear guard. This puzzled me as I knew that we had lost no ground during the day. On inquiry, I found that Lee had sent them about 40,000 reinforcements, while our whole force was only 27,000.

We went 20 miles before they commenced pressing us. At 25 miles our regiment was ordered to check their advance until the train could be moved out of the way. We dismounted and formed our line. The Rebs moved on us with three regiments. We were reinforced by a part of the 14th Pa. Cav. Soon the firing became very brisk. We held them for 1/2 hour when they commenced flanking us and we were ordered to fall back 100 yards where we rallied and again held them until they

The Regimental Band

The original regimental band had been organized with the regiment in the fall of 1861 and served until October 1862 when it was disbanded pursuant to a law passed by Congress abolishing regimental bands as paid auxiliaries of the service. In January 1863 the officers of the regiment raised a fund of $1,000 for purchase of instruments and a new band was recruited from within ranks. Membership in the band consisted of sixteen musicians under the leadership of Andrew Watt who had served in the old band. It was reported that the band was specially honored by General Burnside in the Knoxville campaign.

Later, when the 44th was reorganized into the 8th Ohio Volunteer Cavalry, three additional members were added, and the band served on horseback with the regiment, or on detachment services, throughout the remainder of the war. It reportedly furnished the only music in support of Sheridan's victory at Cedar Creek in October 1864. [11]

flanked us and began delivering a heavy cross fire and we were ordered again to fall back as before.

Although many of us had expended all of our ammunition, we rallied in this way four times after which we were ordered to charge. Although we had neither bayonets or sabres and most of the men had but one round, and many of them not any ammunition at all, not a man faltered. We drove everything before us until, as the rebel line was much longer than ours, they commenced swinging their flanks around and would have captured the whole regiment had we not fallen back.

We lost very heavy in this charge, about 20 killed and wounded. It was now getting dark and we were ordered to retire from the field. I went into the last charge with two rounds of ammunition, held on until I charged some distance when I fired one and held the other in reserve. At the same time, a man was struck dead at my side and the next moment I was struck in the side with a spent ball, inflicting no other injury than a slight scratch that was visible for a few days.

In the whole engagement, our regiment lost about 20 killed and 70 wounded. In our company, the loss was 2 killed, 2 badly wounded left on field and 12 slightly wounded; viz., killed, Albert Elson from Mercer Co. and James Young from near Greenville; wounded and left on field, Corporal John Friday from near Arcanum and John R. Martin from near Uncle Alex Harper's; wounded and taken from field: Corporal Zac Ross, severely in thigh; Sgt. Kerlinger, slightly; Orderly Sgt. Samuel Harrison, in hand; privates Samuel Bishop, Isaac Ross, Albert Hecker, Beverly Penny, Jacob Porter, John Drischman, David F. Swain, Samuel Bennett, Granville M. Arens from Greenville. Several others were struck with spent balls or grazed but not wounded. One half of the men of our company who went into the fight were struck with balls. (There was no artillery used.) This will attest the desperation with which we fought. General Averell complimented us very highly and said it was too good a regiment to be exposed without better arms than we have. He also said we had done fighting enough and relieved us from rear guard.

Lieutenant David Kire was killed instantly, being struck with three balls, one of which entered his breast. Len Langston was slightly wounded. One of the Brant boys was killed and one wounded.

I forbear mentioning the part taken by the 14th Pa. as I could not do it with credit to them.

Our rations had now run out, and we were obliged to ransack the country for a very scanty supply, as you will readily imagine, when you take into consideration that there were 27,000 of us. However, J. Horner, R. Morrison, J. Crick and myself captured enough unbolted flour to last us until two days before we reached supplies, during which time we had nothing. Infantry fared worse as they had less chance to forage. Quite a number of them actually starved to death, probably 20 or 30 or perhaps more. About 400 horses of our regiment gave out and were shot to prevent the Rebs from using them. 135 dead horses were counted within two miles on this side of Lewisburg. We expected to draw rations at Meadow Bluffs, but a regiment of guards which was guarding them was scared by a dozen or so of bushwhackers and burned 200 wagons loaded with rations and beat a hasty retreat for Charleston so we were obliged to go hungry for four more days for their cowardice.

July 3. On arriving at Charleston, we expected to find mail and a detachment that was left here when we started out, but in this we were disappointed. They had all been sent to Martinsburg as our regiment was expected to go there. I understand they are ordered back and that we are to stay in this valley. At any rate, letters directed to Charleston will reach the regiment.

I forgot to mention a very important incident connected with the raid. When we arrived at Salem, the infantry and artillery preceded by the train continued on the march while our division was ordered to check the Rebs until the train could be moved over the Alleghenies. The Rebels kept up a lively skirmish in our rear for an hour when word came that they had flanked us on the right and had cut us off from the column. We were immediately started round to the left at the gallop when near their line we were dismounted and ordered to charge them. They had lit out after making a dash on the artillery capturing four cannon and caissons and 150 horses besides a number of men. General Hunter is severely censured for leaving the artillery unprotected.

We passed a number of places of interest on our route. We

passed two days at White Sulphur Springs, took dinner and passed two hours at Hot Springs, passed Warm Springs, Rockbridge Bath and passed one night at Sweet Springs. The hot springs are quite a curiosity. At the mouth of the springs, the water it is said will boil an egg in 15 minutes. It is cooled by running through pipes and then run into large cisterns for the purpose of bathing. The first cistern is at a temperature of 130 degrees, the next 120, the next 110, the next 100, 90, 80, etc. I bathed in one that was marked 100 degrees. The buildings in some of these places were very costly and elegant, some of them costing 30 or 40 thousand dollars.

Hunter's army is being shipped to Martinsburg fast as possible.

In a letter written at Beverly, West Virginia, dated July 28, 1864, Private Alfred H. Criley, Company I, 8th Ohio Vol. Cav., gave the following account of the Lynchburg campaign:

"I suppose you have heard of our great Lynchburg raid under Gen. Hunter, a nice man he is 'I don't think.' Well, I will not attempt to give you a newspaper account of it but just a little of what we did. We were out thirty-three days, rode thirty out of that time, travelled 700 miles, were in three fights and one skirmish and got back safe. Will that do? This makes six fights and several skirmishes we have taken a hand in.

"Well, to begin we left Charleston on the 28th of May. We travelled over the same old road which we retreated out of the Valley over two years ago. Everything looked as natural as home. We stopped at several of our old camps. At Tompkins Farm we found the old circles where our tents stood before. It seemed but a week since we had been there. I saw our great rock that you spoke of the 'devil's tea table,' and Hawk's Nest. You will recall I described Hawk's Nest to you once. I wish you could see it. We would have 'high talk' then. We reached Lewisburg on the 2nd of June and saw our first battleground. Co. M arrested a man who had killed one of the 8th O.V.C. He was taken along and tried by court martial and acknowledged the crime. Near Warm Springs he was taken out one morning and hung to the limb of a tree near the road and left there as a warning to others. He had a paper pinned on his breast with the word 'for the murder of a Union soldier.' That's the way Gen. Averell serves them. They are more afraid of him than anyone else.

"Don't you think we passed within three miles of the Natural

Bridge and did not get to see it. Isn't that too bad? But we saw the little Blowing Cave in Windy Cove Gap. There is a stream of cold air continuously blowing out of it even in the hottest days. On the 7th of June we passed over the Shenandoah Mountains from the side of which we had a splendid view of the Valley. It is as fine a section of country as I ever saw. Looking from the side of the mountain as far as the eye can reach are beautiful farms with their fields of green dotted with white farm houses and barns. There are the yellow roads, silvery streams, the little towns and ranges of hills, all before you like a map. We could see Gen. Crook's wagon train, with their white covers, like a huge serpent winding its way among the little hills twelve miles distant. We got to Staunton after Hunter had taken the place. At Lexington we saw Stonewall Jackson's grave. From L. we went to Buchanan. Left B. and crossed the Blue Ridge on the top of which our scouts killed a Reb. We saw the highest land in Va. the Peaks of Otter. Passed through Liberty. All the way down to Lynchburg. Was one continual skirmish. The Reb. Gen. McCausland kept just ahead of us fighting and falling back as we advanced.

"On the 17th of June we found the enemy five miles out of Lynchburg, where they had taken position for a fight. Our regiment was sent out as skirmishers to help open the fight. They advanced slowly for some distance when they found the 'Johnnys' in a dense wood. We were relieved by Crook's infantry who opened the fight by a charge on the Rebs. There was some very heavy firing for a little while. After dark we went into camp about a thousand yards in rear of our line, unsaddled, got supper and went to sleep. Several times through the night there was a little fighting in front, just enough to make us think of *tomorrow's work*.

"Saturday, June 18th, got breakfast after sunrise. Moved forward to an old deserted Quaker church and remained there some time. Our lines advanced and drove the Rebs from their first line of entrenchments. The cannonading was very heavy. We were moved farther to the front in rear of our center and held as reserve. The enemy made a desperate assault on our center trying to capture the battery immediately in front of us. The shells fell thick and fast around us but our Regt. had only two wounded there. One shell passed through the 14th Pa. Cav. killing four men and twelve horses. Crook's infantry again met them and repulsed them driving them a mile. Our company was sent out to keep stragglers to the front. We passed a great number of wounded coming to the rear.

"At night we held a mile more ground than in the morning but as the enemy had received 17,000 fresh troops a retreat was ordered and after dark we commenced a retrograde movement.

"Sunday, June 19th. This afternoon our Regt. was halted in Liberty and sent a mile to the rear to check the advance of the enemy. We threw up rail breast works on the brow of a hill near a woods. Co. B was sent forward as skirmishers. They held the woods but a short time when they were driven back onto the reserve. Here they had one man killed. The enemy threw out a full brigade and commenced flanking us. We were ordered to retreat which we did for about 200 yards when we were ordered forward again. We regained the fence but could not hold it long. Here we lost four men. We then retreated to the second fence, across an open field. We held this until the Rebels had us flanked and were pouring in a murderous cross fire. We were then ordered to retreat. We did so until we reached the brow of a hill in our rear. Here we rallied, retook the fence, halted a few minutes, and then charged on the enemy's center driving it back some distance. Here we lost most of our men. The enemy were around us in a horse shoe shape and pouring in a cross fire from every direction except the rear. Most of the boys being out of ammunition we beat a retreat. We were completely exhausted and could not move out of a walk. The Rebels were following and firing on us all the time. We reached the edge of town and were in comparative safety. On the opposite side of town we found the infantry which should have supported us lying idle. The whole affair was poorly managed. We were repeatedly told to hold them just a little longer and we would be reinforced and that the 14 Pa. had gone around to flank them, all of which was false. The loss in our regiment was 79 killed and wounded. We lost several officers. Cap. Winger was wounded in the hand. He is at home now. Our company loss — one killed and ten wounded. We went into camp on the opposite side of town and slept soundly till next morning when we started again on the retreat. We overtook the wagon train and rode all day and all night.

"Tuesday, June 21st. Kept right on without any rest. Reached Salem in the morning. The enemy made an attack on our rear. Our Regt. was sent out to the left of town as skirmishes. The Rebs sent a force around to attack our train. They attacked our artillery in a narrow pass and destroyed 18 pieces and caissons. Our Regt. galloped forward and scattered them in the woods. We crossed Catawba Mountain and encamped 18 miles from Sweet Springs.

"Wednesday, June 22nd. Passed over two very high mountains and encamped at Sweet Springs. Our company was sent out seven miles on picket. From there to this place — there was nothing of importance. We arrived here on June 30th. We have been here nearly a month now and have nothing to do and plenty to eat. We were ordered away from here twice to Webster Station and were ordered back both times after we had made a march of 30 miles.

"Our regiment is all scattered. Part of them are at Parkersburg and part were at Martinsburg before the raid but we don't know where they are now.

"Varshi, if you could see me sitting here in my 'pup' tent, barefooted, trying to keep the flies off and write at the same time you would think I really did prize your letters. Our Quartermaster is not tending to his business and a good many of us have had no boots for three weeks." [12]

From Staunton to Lynchburg, Hunter's army had moved slowly, taking a longer and less direct route and ravaging the countryside along the way. With Lynchburg and its railroad network being vital to the Confederacy, General Lee in a bold move ordered General Jubal Early with 8,000 infantry to move rapidly from the defenses of Richmond to protect Lynchburg from capture. Previously, when Hunter had approached Staunton, General Breckinridge's division of 9,000 men had been sent to resist Hunter's advances. Both Breckinridge and Early reached Lynchburg in time to give battle to Hunter's army. By then the Confederates outnumbered the Federals, and the chance to seize Lynchburg was lost. When a retreat was ordered, Hunter's forces, being short of supplies and ammunition, could do no better than to go west into the mountains, back into the Gauley River Valley and to Charleston. His army was taken out of action for three weeks and left the Shenandoah Valley and the area to the Potomac without adequate defenses.[13]

Commenting on the Lynchburg campaign in his autobiography, General Early had this to say:

"Hunter's delay in advancing from Staunton had been most remarkable. He had defeated Jones' small force at Piedmont, about ten miles from Staunton, on the 5th, and united with Crook on the 8th, yet he did not arrive in front of Lynchburg until near night on the 17th. The route from Staunton to Lynchburg by which he moved, which was by Lexington, Buchanan, the Peaks of Otter and Liberty is about one hundred miles in distance. It is true that McCausland had delayed his progress by keeping constantly in his front, but an energetic advance would have brushed away McCausland's small force, and Lynchburg, with all its manufacturing establishments and stores, would have fallen before assistance arrived.

"Had Hunter moved on Lynchburg with energy, that place would have fallen before it was possible for me to get there. But he tarried on the way, and when he reached there, there was discovered 'a want of ammunition to give battle.'"

General Early also commented on the ravages of Hunter's army:

"The scenes on Hunter's route from Lynchburg had been truly heartrending. Houses had been burned, and women and children left without shelter. The country had been stripped of provisions and many families left without a morsel to eat. — We now had renewed evidences of outrages committed by the commanding general's orders in burning and plundering private homes. We saw the ruins of a number of houses so destroyed. At Lexington Hunter had burned the Military Institute, with all its contents, including the library and scientific apparatus; and Washington College had been plundered and the statue of Washington taken. The residence of Ex-Governor Letcher, at that place had been burned, and but a few minutes given Mrs. Letcher and her family to leave the house. In the same country a Christian gentleman, Mr. Creigh, had been hung because he had killed a straggling and marauding Federal soldier while in the act of insulting and outraging the ladies of his family. The time consumed in the perpetration of those deeds was the salvation of Lynchburg, with its stores, foundries and factories, which were so necessary to our army at Richmond." [14]

And Correspondent Zouave had some thoughts about the retreat from Lynchburg and about the success of the raid:

"Colonels Schoonmaker's brigade, the 14th Pennsylvania, and the 8th O.V.C., covered the retreat. Sunday evening the rebels attached the command in force. The 8th and a battalion of the 14th Pennsylvania held the front line. The rebels deployed two regiments as skirmishers, supported by a brigade, and advanced. The shock fell on the front line. Nobly it met and repelled the charged. The 8th outdone even the fighting of the old 44th. —

"Why the 8th was not supported is, in the language of a general officer, useless to inquire. Their fighting was most gallant, and was not thrown away. In the third charge made by the regiment, the one when it had no ammunition — nothing save the bare carbine, the promise was that Colonel Powell's brigade should charge on the right, and another on the left, but they failed to come to time. The fight taught our cavalry one truth — our carbines are worthless. Not a man can say he hit a rebel. After a few times the powder would burn out the chamber. Full one-fourth would not snap a cap the first time. — Such is the arm, and the only one, the 8th O.V.C. is armed with. The men knew the worthlessness of their weapon, yet for hours they stood up against a brigade of four regiments, charged it three times, and beat it back each time. What would not a regiment do if effectively armed? —

"What was the expedition? — A regular movement or a raid? If the former, it was an utter failure; — if the latter, it didn't pay. We destroyed more artillery, ammunition, horses and horse equipments, and mules, than the enemy was damaged. Besides the loss of men killed, wounded and captured. The whole army suffered for want of a system." [15]

Parkersburg, West Virginia
July 12, 1864

I wrote you a letter on our arrival at Charleston containing an account of our raid. I also stated that our mail had been sent to Martinsburg. It was all sent back to Charleston and arrived there two days after I wrote to you. I received ten letters, including one from Jennie dated June 1st containing two photos and one from you dated June 3 also containing two photos and the p. stamps.

Speaking of photos reminds me that I had the misfortune of having my album either lost or stolen. It contains 18 photos. It was lost while on the raid. In your next, please send me one of your own if you have it to spare and the one of Miss _____ which I left with you.

Our regiment is now divided in three detachments. We left 200 men at Charleston without horses. They were sent to the Army of the Potomac, and I understand were ordered to draw infantry arms but we have not heard anything definite from them. S. Myers and Creeger are with that detachment.

When two miles from Lewisburg, our regiment was ordered to send all sick and those who had played-out horses with the column and was then sent back in the direction we had come. That is the last we have seen or heard of them. I think they went through to Beverly or Martinsburg and that we are now awaiting transportation on the R.R. to join them. I was sent back from Lewisburg because a lieutenant in the 7th Va. Cavalry had stolen my horse the night before, and I was then mounted on a worn-out horse that was not able for a hard march. I found my horse the next day.

The troops are nearly all being sent from Kanawha Valley to Martinsburg fast as they can get transportation for them. The infantry is sent by water to this place, then by rail. Cavalry and artillery are sent here by land when they also go by rail.

In regard to Colonel Gilbert, he always had a few enemies in the regiment but before he gave our company the cursing, 3/4 of them or more were strongly in favor of him. A petition was circulated and signed by all who were not on drill to have him remain with the regiment. After the company came in and the men found how he had used the men who were out, they demanded the petition and tore it up. So you see the opinion of the company was turned by the one act. Had he been in command at Liberty, I have no idea he would have allowed us to be exposed as we were. Other companies went for him almost unanimous and even our company have nearly all begun to wish he commanded the regiment. So you see how unstable men are in their opinion. I have always been a strong Gilbert man. Creeger was not yet a lieutenant but expected a commission and would have in all probability received it soon had he not been reduced.

News has just come that our whole regiment was captured at or near Beverly. Our informant (a citizen) says, "they fought like hell before giving up." Of course, we will not believe it until it is well authenticated. But I will have to close with this as we will leave here in a day or two and I have nine more answers to write.

Following the retreat from Lynchburg the regiment was divided, one detachment being sent to Beverly, West Virginia and the other taking part in the operations in the Shenandoah Valley. The regiment remained separated until December 1, 1864.[16]

John McKee's friend, William H. Creeger, died July 13, 1864, at Harpers Ferry of wounds received in action.[17]

The itinerary of the detachment serving in the Valley campaign (1st Brigade, 2nd Cavalry Division, Army of West Virginia) as listed in Dyer's Compendium of the War of the Rebellion is as follows:

July 22	—	Battle of Winchester or Kernstown, Va.
July 25	—	Engagement Martinsburg, West Va.
July 29	—	Hagerstown, Md.
July 31	—	Hancock, Md.
July 31	—	McConnelsburg, Pa.
Aug. 26	—	Williamsport, Pa.
Aug. 31	—	Action, Martinsburg, West Va.
Sept. 2-3	—	Action, Bunker Hill, West Va.
Sept. 10	—	Skirmish, Darkesville, West Va.
Sept. 13	—	Bunker Hill, West Va.
Sept. 14	—	Skirmish, near Berryville, Va.
Sept. 18	—	Action, near Martinsburg, West Va.
Sept. 22	—	Battle of Opequan, Winchester, Va.
Sept. 22	—	Battle of Fisher's Hill, Va.
Sept. 22-23	—	Action, Mt. Jackson, Va.
Sept. 24	—	Skirmish, Forest Hill or Timberville, Va.
Sept. 28	—	Skirmish, Port Republic, Va.
Oct. 6	—	Skirmish, North Shenandoah, Va.
Oct. 7	—	Skirmish, Luray Valley, Va.
Oct. 19	—	Battle of Cedar Creek, Va.
Oct. 20	—	Skirmish, Dry Run, Va.
Oct. 25-26	—	Skirmishes, Milford, Va.
Nov. 12	—	Action, Ninevah, Va.
Nov. 22	—	Action, Rude's Hill near Mt. Jackson, Va.

Newcreek, Virginia
August 10, 1864

It has been some time since I last wrote you, but we have been on the move constantly since then so that I have not had time to write sooner. When I wrote you last from Parkersburg, I said we were under orders for Martinsburg. We were sent from there to Winchester and were in the advance when we were so badly repulsed by the Rebs.

We were deployed as dismounted skirmishers with a column of cavalry in our rear. Soon as the Rebs appeared on our flanks, the cavalry broke on the run while our regiment had to retreat on foot and had to go five miles before we found our horses. Several from our regiment were captured (two of our company) and we would all have been taken had not the 1st Va. Cavalry taken us on their horses behind them. This was a most complete rout and we lost heavily, mostly infantry with four pieces of artillery.

At Martinsburg, we made a stand and drove their cavalry out of town after they had taken possession of it. We fought here mounted, lost two horses, had one man wounded slightly. We then fell back to Hagerstown, Md. While there, we were encamped near the regiment Will Horner belongs to. I saw him several times. He is a 1st lieutenant and will soon be a captain. He belongs to the 2nd Md. Cavalry. James Horner procured a pass to go to see some of his relations living nine miles from there and had not returned when the Rebels took the place on their way to Pennsylvania. We have not heard from him since. On this raid, they made a feint on Hagerstown from Williamsport with a column of infantry while their cavalry pushed from Clear Springs to Chambersburg.

As soon as General Averell became aware of their intentions, he endeavored to head them by going around via Greencastle, Berryville (I believe that is the name) and Fayetteville. We passed four miles to the right of Chambersburg, most of the way through fields and by roads. We stopped at Fayetteville for dinner. I took dinner with James Horner. They all seemed very glad to see me.

I never saw such a sight as was presented at Chambersburg. Women and children that two hours before had not known what it was to want for anything were now standing around the ruins of their once happy homes with nothing left but the clothing they had on. The whole town was burned except a few houses in the suburbs.

We did not stop in town but pushed on after the Rebs. Captured five of them one mile from town. At the request of the citizens, they were sent back and delivered over to them. They were made short work of and thrown on the red hot ruins of some of the houses. The citizens were so exasperated they nearly killed one Reb before the guards delivered them over.

We then pursued them to McConnelsburg, thence to Hancock where they tried to cross the river but we pushed them too close. After a sharp skirmish, they pushed on to Cumberland and Newcreek. We rested there two days and

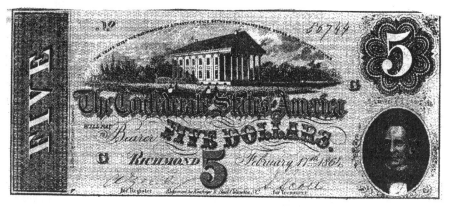

Confederate money "captured" at Moorefield, West Virginia, and sent home by John McKee

started in pursuit via Springfield and Romeny. We overtook them at Moorefield where we had the nicest cavalry fight I ever saw.

We captured their pickets during the night, moved on them at daybreak taking them completely by surprise so much so that one brigade encamped on this side of the river had not time to form a line. A division on the other side formed a hasty line but it was soon broken. They outnumbered us and would have whipped us in a fair fight. We took their artillery (four pieces) before they had time to fire a shot. The Rebs had been told by their general that we would take no prisoners from that command. This influenced them to fight with the utmost desperation. Many of them would not surrender and were cut down with the sabre or shot at a distance of four or five paces. Several of the artillerymen jumped on their guns and refused to surrender and were shot.

Our loss was seven killed, 21 wounded. Our regiment had one wounded. The Rebel loss was 450 prisoners and about 200 killed and wounded. We captured about 1,000 horses.

Our division needed something of this kind to revive the spirits of the men. We have been going constantly for the last three months without gaining any victory worth mentioning and the men had begun to get out of heart. This has had a great influence towards that end.

I have not received a letter from you since I wrote a letter from Charleston. If you sent the money I requested, I have not received it but expect it is at Beverly with the regiment. I

Moorefield, West Virginia, August 7, 1864

need it now as I captured a horse at Moorefield and sold it for $30. The horse was worth $150, but that was all I could get for it.

I suppose we will leave for Martinsburg tomorrow. I send you some Rebel money I captured at Moorefield. Some of the men captured a large amount of money, gold, silver and greenbacks.

Shepherdstown, Virginia
August 19, 1864
We have until 4 p.m. to write letters when they will be taken away by courier.

After leaving Hankup, we went to Martinsburg where we were promised 30 days rest but yesterday morning at 2 a.m. we were ordered to get ready to march. We soon learned that Early had been reinforced by two army corps and that Sheridan was falling back in the direction of Harpers Ferry, followed by the Rebel infantry while their cavalry were reported moving in the direction of Martinsburg.

We arrived here last evening where we are bivouacked in line of battle awaiting to hear of the movement of the Rebs or possibly to prevent the Rebs crossing a ford at this place across the Potomac. We are in sight of the Antietam battleground although it is on the opposite side of the river on the Maryland side. We are within 11 miles of Harpers Ferry.

It is hard to tell what will be the result of this movement but direct to Averell's Division at Harpers Ferry.

Near Bunker Hill, Virginia
September 5, 1864
I believe I wrote to you last from Sharpsburg if I am not mistaken. Since that, we as usual have been moving most of the time.

We went from Sharpsburg to Hagerstown and the next day the Rebs tried to cross the river at Williamsport when we were sent there to reinforce that post. The Rebs, finding they could not cross, retreated and we followed them as far as Martinsburg and were in turn driven out of there the second day after. We went to the Potomac at Williamsport but did not cross it. The next day we followed the Rebs through Martinsburg to six miles on this side where we came upon a division of their cavalry. We charged them and drove them five miles on the run, capturing 20 wagons and about 40 prisoners. But here we run into a large force of their infantry and had to fall back to Big Springs, a distance of five miles. The next day they made a charge on us but we were ready for them and drove them back to Bunker Hill faster than they came. Finding their infantry, we returned to Big Springs with only a small loss.

The next day (yesterday) the Rebs left Bunker Hill and we followed them after night to near Winchester where we very unexpectedly run nearly into 30,000 infantry. General Averell had been informed they had fallen back past Winchester and the first intimation of them was the sight of their campfires when we were nearly on to them. We immediately turned about and went three miles where we are now in line of battle ready to follow them up in case they fall back further or to retreat if they advance on us too heavily.

In the last week, I have been in three charges besides some skirmishing. Cavalry is the most exciting as well as the safest branch of the service. Since the Lynchburg raid, our company has done a great deal of fighting but has not lost a man either killed or wounded and only one captured; viz., our 1st Lieutenant John Babb who was captured on the 3rd while on picket with 10 men, none of which belonged to our company. Henry McCowen's horse was wounded twice on the first of the month. Scipio Myers came near being captured on the 3rd. The rebs were driving the part of the line in which he was. He went to leap a ditch when his horse fell and by the time he remounted the Rebs were within 50 yards of him. They fired more than 50 shots at him but he escaped unhurt. I think we will occupy Winchester tomorrow as it is the impression that the Rebs are falling back slowly out of the valley.

We have received news of the Chicago convention. The Butternut ticket will be more popular with the soldiers this fall than last as it offers an armistice or peace, either of which is tempting to a soldier who has served three years and is getting tired of the war. McClellan is an officer in the army which is a good cloak to hide his Butternut principles.

We have not had our saddles off our horses for two weeks.

*In the field near
Bunker Hill, Virginia
September 7, 1864*

We were ordered out before I had time to mail this letter and will now add to it before sending. I said we were ordered out. It was to make a reconnaissance to ascertain if the Rebs had withdrawn their infantry. To do this, we have to drive their cavalry about three miles and the first we seen of their infantry they were on our left flank and their cavalry on our right, nearly on our rear. They delivered a heavy enfilading fire into us but we retired in good order with slight loss.

It rained heavily the whole time. Yesterday we drove in their advance skirmish line and they drove ours in last night. We fell back five miles and are now seven miles from Martinsburg.

Simon Trowbridge of our company had his horse shot from under him yesterday.

*Leestown, Virginia
September 9, 1864*

I wrote you a letter yesterday but think I lost it before mailing it, or at least do not remember putting it in the office. At all events, I will write today so that you will be sure to hear from me since writing from Shepherdstown, Md.

We have been in four engagements. First, we were driven out of Martinsburg to the river. Second, we charged the Rebels and drove them five miles on the run when they fell back on their infantry at Bunker Hill when we fell back four miles.

The next day, they attacked us but we were ready for them and drove them back faster than they came. The fourth, we made a reconnaissance in force to find whether their infantry was at Winchester or not. To do this, we had to drive their cavalry about two miles. After we drove them back, the first we saw of their infantry they were on each side of us trying to surround us. But we discovered them just in time and withdrew.

I was in several other skirmishes while scouting. The pickets have been skirmishing nearly all the time for the last week. Henry McCowen had his horse shot twice at Martinsburg. Simon Trowbridge had his shot on a picket reconnaissance and Hecker had his shot near Winchester. In

A cavalry charge, September 1864

going from Martinsburg to Winchester (22 miles) one scarcely gets out of sight of horses that have been shot in action. In some places, 10 or 12 or even more can be counted from the same place.

Cavalry fighting is the most exciting as well as the safest branch of the service. It is impossible for a mounted man to take good aim and, under as heavy a fire as infantry is sometimes subjected to, cavalry would soon have nearly all their horses shot when they would be noneffective.

Our 1st Lieutenant John H. Babb was captured while on picket with four men, neither of which belonged to our company.

We have been moving constantly or encamped in line of battle with our saddles on ready for action for the last three weeks until today. We have unsaddled and are resting although we are liable to be called out any moment.

I wish you could see some of our charges. It is an imposing scene to see one line of cavalry a mile long rush on to another of equal size and then when they break, to see the two lines, one pursued by the other, shooting and yelling like Indians. Occasionally, part of the line will get behind a stone fence or in good position and make a stand, but it is only the work of a moment to reenforce that part of the line and compel them to leave it.

A few days ago, we received an account of the proceedings of the Chicago convention. Let others say as they will. The Butternut ticket will be more popular with the soldiers this fall than it was last unless our armies meet with some unprecedented success before the election comes off. They offer as an inducement peace or at least an armistice, either of which are very enticing to one who has been fighting three years and is tired of the war. Many of the veterans reenlisted under the impression that the war would certainly close this fall. They now find that although we have been very successful in most cases, movements this summer the close of the war is set as usual about six months ahead by the knowing ones. I am not getting disheartened. I never allow myself to get despondent. I only give you the general tone of the army.

Hagerstown, Maryland
September 11, 1864

I came here yesterday in charge of 50 worn-out horses of our regiment. Will probably stay here six or eight days. Our regiment was in a fight yesterday, and I hear it was badly cut up but not from a reliable source.

Hagerstown, Maryland
September 12, 1864

I wrote you a few days ago, but as I have changed my base of operations, I thought I would write you a line to keep you posted. I have been detailed as Q.M. Sergeant of the dismounted camp at this place. There is at present about 800 men of our division dismounted and they are kept here until equipped and sent to the front. It is a very good position and is similar to a clerkship. I am stationed here permanently.

Hagerstown, Maryland
September 21, 1864

I am still with the Q.M. and am very well pleased with the place. The regiment is still doing its accustomed amount of fighting. They lost 20 prisoners one day last week in a fight at Martinsburg. We also lost our adjutant in the same fight. I have not heard from our company since the engagement and do not know what its loss is.

Averell's division took a very important part in Sheridan's great battle of the 19th. Sheridan's recent victories in the valley and Sherman's glorious campaign have had a wonderful effect in the army in regard to the election. Little Mc is losing favor very rapidly. The 11th Virginia Infantry passed through Hagerstown last evening enroute for Sheridan's army. They were very loud in their demonstrations for Lincoln. If the army meets with no important reverse until the election, the soldiers' vote will be a great deal more unanimous than I expected it would a week ago.

The photos came to hand alright. I am obliged to you for sending them.

John McKee's assessment of the support that President Lincoln had among the soldiers was correct. Although the President would have won without the soldier vote, his margin of victory would not have been as great. The vote was also decisive in several congressional elections. The four-to-one vote in favor of the President over General McClellan was an impressive mandate for the President to continue the war until the South was defeated.

Remount Camp
Pleasant Valley, Maryland
November 17, 1864

I received yours of the 9th (I believe) containing $10 for which I am truly thankful although I will not be able to spend it riding out with the ladies of Hagerstown as we left there more than a week ago.

I was sadly disappointed when the order came to leave (Hagerstown) as it was generally supposed that we would remain there all winter.

I never enjoyed myself better anywhere than I did there. Whist or Euchre parties almost every evening and riding out horseback almost every day. So you see, I put in the time very pleasantly. We are now two miles from Harpers Ferry and 21 miles from Hagerstown. This is the most desolate place I have seen for a long time. The valley is almost 1/2 mile wide, while the mountains rise on each side and 3/4 of a mile in front (across the river) almost perpendicular to a height which seem to say "thus far thou shalt to and no further."

There are two or three thousand dismounted cavalry camped here and there has always been troops encamped here since the beginning of the war. You will not wonder then that the country around (what there is of it) presents a desolate appearance. I have made application to go to the regiment at Beverly, but think it extremely doubtful whether I get to go or not. Doubtless, you have heard the particulars of the fight they have had there some time ago. It was a most brilliant affair. They were attacked while at roll call in the morning by about an equal number of Rebs and were run out of camp before some of them could get their arms. They retreated to a hill where they rallied. Those that had no arms, took clubs and stones. They then went at them in earnest. Took 120 prisoners. Killed and wounded quite a number, although they lost quite heavily themselves. We had 15 killed. In Co. G, the loss was three killed, viz., Sgt. Galloway, Harvey Byers and Asa

Sackman and four wounded.

An officer of a Maryland Regiment told at Hagerstown that he saw three rebels that were killed with clubs and stones. This account is probably inaccurate in some things as I was not there and have had no opportunity to get the particulars from those who were engaged. I expect to go to Hagerstown on a visit in a few days if I don't go to Beverly.

The surprise attack on the outpost at Beverly, West Virginia where the other detachment of the 8th Ohio was stationed resulted in an utter failure. Another description of the events was later written by historian Whitelaw Reid, in his works entitled *Ohio in the War: Her Statesmen, Her Generals, and Soldiers*.

"With now and then a scout, the regiment rested quietly until the 9th of October, when three hundred Rebels dashed into camp, just before daylight, intending a surprise. Fortunately the men were all up, and some of the companies were falling in for roll call; and when the firing at the pickets was heard the men seized their carbines and formed behind the horse-racks, and were able for a time to check the advance; but the Rebels came in by the flank and rear, and it soon became a hand-to-hand conflict, the men fighting by squads, by couples, and singly, with carbines clubbed, and in some instances grappling without weapons, and endeavoring to strangle each other. Near the officers' quarters a party was collected, and charged a portion of the Rebels twice, scattering them in all directions. About this time the Rebel leader, Major Hill, of the Sixty-Second Virginia Infantry, was shot by one of our scouts, who was just returning. The rebels, seeing their leader fall, fled, but were closely pursued, and nearly all the prisoners they had taken released. The rout was complete, the Rebels losing seventeen killed, twenty-seven wounded, and ninety-two prisoners, while the regiment lost only eight killed, twenty-five wounded, and thirteen prisoners." [18]

Remount Camp
Pleasant Valley, Maryland
December 27, 1864
Christmas is over and I did not get to go to Hagerstown. The other two clerks were detailed to go to General Torbert's Headquarters, which threw the responsibility of the office on me so that I could not get off. It was a dry Christmas to me as there is no source of amusement here.

Christmas 1864. Pleasant Valley, Maryland

> *We have had several inches of snow and very good sleighing for more than a week until last night when it went off with a rain. As you will readily imagine, the merry ringing of sleigh bells was well calculated to awaken thoughts of home and home pleasures. I hope I will not be compelled to pass another Christmas in the army. Sherman has given the Rebs a blow that will tell heavily on them.*

The year 1864 had been a mixed bag for the men of the regiment. It had started off on a high note with the regiment's reorganization into a cavalry unit and most of the men reenlisting. The furlough and the celebration at Springfield had been memorable enough. Although they engaged in pillaging on the raid to Lynchburg, they conducted themselves admirably in covering the retreat of Hunter's Army. From then on they were divided, with part of the regiment stationed at Beverly, West Virginia, and the other participating in the Shenandoah campaign. The detachment at Beverly under Lieutenant Colonel Youart withstood a surprise attack at that outpost in October. The detachment in the Shenandoah, under Colonel Moore, was engaged in several major battles and skirmishes. Both groups performed well enough to be proud of their record while under fire. It is apparent, however, that they suffered for lack of leadership, for want of proper equipment and arms and because they were separated.

In November, General W.H. Powell, who had succeeded General Averell as the 2nd Cavalry Division Commander, requested that the detachment of the 8th Ohio numbering about 160 men be returned to the regiment. He stated that much dissatisfaction was felt among the men on account of the separation and that more service would be obtained from the regiment by its being complete in its organization. In forwarding General Powell's request, the division commander recommended that it be granted, stating that the regiment in its present condition was almost worthless, and since a request to bring the Beverly contingent east had been refused, it would be in best interests of the service that the regiment be consolidated in Beverly. On November 26, 1864, General Sheridan ordered that the men of the detachment be relieved of their duty and to proceed to join the remainder of the regiment at Beverly.

The end of the year also marked trouble for the regiment's young colonel, A.S. Moore, who had succeeded Colonel Gilbert. When the 44th was first organized in September 1861, Moore was captain of

Company A. In May of 1863 he was promoted to Major, and when the regiment reorganized, he became Lieutenant Colonel at age 25 and soon thereafter was promoted to the rank of colonel, to step into "Old Sammy's shoes" as Correspondent Zouave had stated it. Following the Lynchburg campaign, Colonel Moore was in charge of the detachment that served with the 2nd Cavalry Division, first under Averill and later under Brig. Gen. W.H. Powell. Late in the fall numerous charges were lodged against Colonel Moore by Lt. Colonel Youart which resulted in Moore's arrest pending court martial. Although there is no evidence of rivalry, jealousy or animosity between the two officers, one suspects that there may have been a divisive relationship between them. In fact, it may have been Youart's appointment to the field that had prompted Colonel Gilbert's resignation. In one of his letters to the newspaper Colonel Gilbert pointed out that Captain Youart had given his influence against reenlistment and that his company had reenlisted under Lieut. Allen. Colonel Gilbert asked, "When he declined to try to reenlist his company, or to participate in the efforts to reenlist the regiment — do you wonder that his promotion under these circumstances is opposed?"

Charges against Colonel Moore arose out of alleged activities involving the sale of captured horses; the failure to timely process muster roll papers and other documents; diversion of regimental baggage and official papers to the front rather than to Beverly, and conduct unbecoming an officer and a gentleman. In one specification, it was alleged that while intoxicated he had caused his brigade and regiment to be turned out as if to repel an attack of the enemy without orders and without an alarm, the men crying as they moved out and back, "Black Hawk is drunk. Apple Jack! Apple Jack!" His brigade was recalled by General Powell, the division commander. Another specification accused him with two other officers with being in the company of two notorious women whom they were escorting in a military ambulance. It was alleged that the women were smoking and swearing and the Colonel was drunk. When the vehicle was stopped at the advance guard line pursuant to orders not allowing any vehicle to pass, the Colonel ordered the guard to let go the horses and swore if he did not he would be "God-damned if he would not blow his (the Sergeant's) brains out."

On November 10, 1864, Colonel Moore was released from arrest to assume command of his regiment; Lt. Colonel Youart continued to forward charges against him, and the matter was placed before a court martial. On January 3, 1865, Colonel Moore tendered resignation of his commission, stating that his retiring from the service was urged by the Governor of Ohio in a manner which would make it impossible under any circumstances to retain command of the regiment either with credit to himself or advantage to the service. He further stated, "I am in receipt of a letter from the Adjutant General of Ohio in which he states that my vindication before a court martial will in no way change the opinion of the Governor in regard to my merits as an officer. Under the circumstances, I do not feel called upon to defend myself, since if successful the final result will not be materially changed." It is interesting to note that in reviewing the matter, the departmental commander, Major General George Crook, stated, "I am led to believe that the charges cannot be substantiated, and the best interests of the service will be promoted by permitting him to resign." On January 4, 1865, he was honorably discharged from service.[19]

But the regiment was uniting again for the first time in months. On December 26th, John McKee and ten others who had been stationed at the Remount Camp, Pleasant Valley, Maryland, were ordered to report to their regiment for duty without delay.

While 1864 may have been a full year for the regiment and many of its men had in fact "seen the elephant," the new year would be destined to be disastrous for them. They will have one more fateful chance to see it again.

1865

Escape from capture, Beverly, West Virginia
January 11, 1865

1865

Buckhannon, West Virginia
July 12, 1864
[January 12, 1865]

You have doubtless heard of our fight at Beverly and are anxious to know how I fared. I will tell you.

I arrived there at dark of the evening previous to the fight. The next morning at 4 a.m., one of the boys woke me up and told me the camp was attacked. I jumped up, put on one of my boots and one of Daniel Eirsman's, found my overcoat and hat and started for the stable 50 yards distant to get my horse. Saw a squad of men around the stable and as it was dark supposed they were our own men. They demanded to know who I was. I said I belonged to the 8th Ohio and was going on to get my horse when a half dozen revolvers were drawn on me and I was demanded to surrender.

You can judge my surprise and of my reflections when I began to think of Libby prison, Belle Isle, etc. They then ordered me to go in the stable and hand out the horses to them. I noticed the column was moving on and, although the men hurried me up and had a revolver bearing on me all the time, I was as slow bout it as possible. After I handed him out two horses, I noticed the column was about 20 paces off. Thinking he had his hands full and couldn't shoot very fast, I started for our lines which were some distance off.

Several shots were fired at me, one of which wounded me very slightly on the top of the right shoulder. It was by a pistol ball and made two holes in my coat about two inches apart. It just entered the skin. As you will readily imagine, I made good time until I crossed the bridge. Soon after, the Rebs burned it to keep our men from crossing.

All of the 8th Ohio and 34th Ohio, except 150 who crossed the river, are supposed to be captured. We arrived here the next evening, a distance of 30 miles, almost worn out. The 34th were all captured but about 30 men, the 8th all but about 120. Company G lost 60 men; 20 escaped. Only four of our officers escaped, viz., Capt. Evans, Capt. Petit, Lt. Potter and Lt. Dalton. I send you a list of those of our company who are supposed to be captured.

I intended to send a communication to the journal, but Lt. Potter thought I had better wait until we would see whether none of the company would not come in. Please send me some money as I have lost everything and am boarding out at 50 cts. per week besides rations. I have a very nice place to board. I lost about 30 dollars worth of clothing, etc. Send by S. Myers if you can or by mail. $15 will do.

    Captain McAlpine   S. Hahn
    1st Sergeant S. Harrison   Henry Huls
    1st Sergeant J.E. Harrison   Samuel Hays
    1st Sergeant W.H. Robbins   William Inman
    1st Sergeant J.S. Ross   F.L. Johnson
    Corporal Samuel Bishop   Elijah Kring
        Isaac Ross   D. Locker
        William Granger   William A. Martin
        J. Corbin   M.L. Hall
    Privates G. Arens   J. Moldin
        G. Adam   I. Mote
        Henry Bierly   Henry McCowen
        Harvey Bierly   B. Penny
        John Barrack   J.K. Porter
        Alanson Byers   S.H. Ross
        Stephen Byers   E.O. Reck
        J. Crick   Fred. Renthler
        John Drischman   Henry Snider
        Charles Flemming   H. Smith
        Jacob Folkerth   George Shields
        L.D. Folkerth   Robert Thompson
        William Folkerth   G. Taylor
        J.G. Galloway   J. Taylor
        John Graham   William Teagarden
        T.B. Gower   Simon Trowbridge
        B. Harper   William Wiekle
        B. Hurley   Alf. Wiekle
        James Horner   Ira M. Wilson

Upon hearing of the surprise attack on Beverly, Major General George Crook, the departmental commander, sent two "trusty staff officers" to examine into and report upon the affair. On January 20, 1865, Colonel Nathan Wilkinson, of the Sixth West Virginia Infantry made the following report:

"Hdqrs. First Brig., Second Infty. Div., Dept. of W. Va.,
Clarksburg, W.Va., January 20, 1865

"Captain: In obedience to the request of the general commanding the Department of West Virginia, I accompanied Capt. J.L. Botsford and Lieut. Benjamin H. Moore of his staff to assist in investigating and reporting upon the facts connected with the late disaster of the U.S. troops stationed at Beverly, W. Va., January 11, 1865, and under immediate command of Lieut. Col. Robert Youart, Eighth Ohio Volunteer Cavalry. The officers of the commanding general's staff will make their report direct to him, and I herewith submit, for the consideration and information of the general commanding the Second Infantry Division, Department of West Virginia, the following (accompanying this is a diagram of the post of Beverly and country near it):

"The pickets during the day were posted as follows: At Russell's, on the Philippi road, a corporal and three men; at the burnt bridge on Buckhannon road, in town, a corporal and three men; and sentinels at the points numbered on the diagram 2, 3, and 4. At dark the pickets were withdrawn from Russell's and the burnt bridge, and in their stead single sentinels were posted at the point marked No. 1 and blacksmith shop. These night sentinels were respectively about 400 yards from camp, and Nos. 1, 2, 3, and 4 were about 300 yards from each other, and all were relieved from camp every two hours. The enemy, about 700 mounted men, wearing U.S. greatcoats, under General Rosser, came in from Crab Bottom, by the Staunton and Beverly pike. At the foot of Cheat Mountain they left the pike and took a road leading on the east side of the Valley River to a point marked A on the diagram, and made a detour around the camp and town on an old dirt road, and formed their line of battle in a hollow, marked B on the diagram, and within 450 yards of the camp. The sentinel at the point marked No. 3 on the diagram saw the rebels approaching and challenged them, who comes there? The reply was, "Friends." He moved toward them and was captured. The first intimation our forces had of the presence of the enemy was the rebels forcing the doors of the quarters, demanding a surrender. This was first at the quarters of the Thirty-fourth Ohio Infantry. The surprise was complete; our forces did not have time to rally even one company together. Quite a number of officers of both regiments were examined, and all testified that they had repeatedly called the attention of the commanding officers to the insufficiency of the guard for picket duty. Lieutenant-Colonel Youart himself states that owing to the severity of the weather, the high water in the rivers, and the statements of the citizens "that it was impossible for the enemy to attack at that time of the year," he felt perfectly secure.

"After the attack of Major Hall on Beverly, October 29, 1864, a camp guard of 100 men was placed on duty, but was relieved by Major Souders, Eighth Ohio Volunteer Cavalry, on account of the cold weather, and his thinking there was no necessity for the guard at this season of the year. Lieutenant-Colonel Youart states that this guard was relieved without his orders.

"Major Butters, Thirty-fourth Ohio Volunteer Infantry, testified that he notified Lieutenant-Colonel Furney, of the same regiment, that the guard was insufficient, and if they (the forces) were attacked they would be captured. At that time Lieutenant-Colonel Furney was in command at Beverly during the absence of Lieutenant-Colonel Youart at Cumberland, Md. Lieutenant-Colonel Youart returned from Cumberland and resumed command two days before the attack by General Rosser. The testimony was that all the officers of the Thirty-fourth Ohio Volunteer Infantry were quartered in town — not one with the regiment — and it has been unofficially reported to me that on the evening previous to the attack there was a ball in the town, which was largely attended by officers, who remained there until a late hour of the night. From the evidence produced it appears that the whole command was latterly in a loose state of discipline.

"In connection with this report, I would respectfully call attention to the fact that the Thirty-fourth Ohio Volunteer Infantry were at Beverly without any official knowledge on my part of their having been sent to that post. My first intimation of their presence at Beverly was from Lieutenant-Colonel Youart, who telegraphed me that they have arrived. Lieutenant-Colonel Furney made no reports to these headquarters, although requested by me to do so. The Thirty-fourth Ohio Volunteer Infantry claims to belong to the command of Brigadier-General Duval, and, I am unofficially informed, reported to him.

"The losses of the command were as follows: Eighth Ohio Volunteer Cavalry — killed, 5; wounded, 17; prisoners, 6 officers and

332 men. Thirty-fourth Ohio Volunteer Infantry — killed, 1; wounded, 6; prisoners, 2 officers and 240 men. Total killed, wounded, and missing, 609.

"The losses were in horses over 100, including the officers' and quartermaster's horses; in quartermaster stores, very small; in commissary stores, about 10,000 rations complete. In arms and equipments, I estimate the loss of the Thirty-fourth Ohio Volunteer Infantry at 250 arms and 300 equipments, and of the Eighth Ohio Volunteer Cavalry at 390 arms and equipments for about 300 men.

"The number of men of the Eighth Ohio Volunteer Cavalry now at Philippi is 381, and of the Thirty-fourth Ohio Volunteer Infantry is 115. Total number of arms of all kinds, 241, and 36 sabers, and nearly 20 rounds of ammunition to the man.

"On arrival at Philippi I took immediate measures to have ammunition sent from Clarksburg, and instructed Lieutenant-Colonel Youart to promptly make requisition for arms for his regiment.

"Owing to the late disaster, and the fact that many of the men now at Philippi are unarmed, the condition of the troops there is very loose and unsatisfactory.

"After a careful examination I can not but come to the conclusion that the disaster was the result of a laxity of discipline, carelessness, and insufficiency of guard." [1]

Also on the 20th Lt. Col. Youart requested that a court of inquiry be instituted relative to the surprise attack which request was disapproved by Major General Crook on the 28th stating, "This matter has been thoroughly and effectually investigated." On that date, General Crook forwarded to headquarters for the Middle Military Division the report of Colonel Wilkinson along with his own recommendation that Lt. Col. Youart and Lt. Col. Furney be dismissed from service for disgraceful neglect of their commands and for permitting themselves to be surprised and the greater portion of their commands captured. On February 4th, Major General Sheridan ordered their dismissal subject to approval of the President and on February 21st the order was confirmed.

The Union casualties at Beverly were reported to be 6 killed, 23 wounded and 580 captured.[2] The captured men were taken to Richmond, Va., where they were held as prisoners until February 15, 1865, when they were sent to Annapolis, Md., and thence to Camp Chase (Parole Camp), Ohio, where they were mustered out by order of the War Department.[3]

Philippi, West Virginia
February 7, 1865

I wrote to you from Buckhannon on the 12th of last month and have been looking for an answer for some time, but have not heard from you yet. I have just learned that all letters that were sent from that place at the same time were very slow in reaching their destination. This being the case, if you have written lately, I will in all probability get the letter although it may be directed to Buckhannon. I requested some money. If you have not sent it, I would like for you to send $15.00 to this place soon as you can.

I will not give you a description of the fight at Beverly until I hear whether you received my other letter or not as I gave details in that. I expect to get a detail in the regimental Q.M. department tomorrow.

I have been doing very well since we came here. Very little duty and am boarding out at $1.00 per week besides rations.

It snows three and melts one day out of four here or has since I came here.

Major Shaw has rejoined the regiment and is in command of the post at Weston about 30 miles from here. I have not seen him yet.

Philippi, West Virginia
February 17, 1865

I think the adage "better late than never" is peculiarly adapted to your case. Why did you not write sooner.

I suppose you think you have a good joke on me for dating my letter in July instead of January. Well, it is pretty good I'd admit but I wrote in a great hurry and should not be held responsible for trifling mistakes.

I find that people at home place a great deal too much importance in the "dancing trap" as you term it. It is true that there was a dance in the town within 300 yards of camp, but instead of having been gotten up at the instigation of any of the Rebel citizens, it was entirely gotten up by the officers of our regiment as an introductory to those of the 34th Ohio who had arrived only a few days previous. Some of them may have been drunk, very likely they were, but at all events the dance was broken up and every man in his quarters several hours before the attack was made.

I have reason to believe that none of our pickets were relieved by any of the Rebels although a portion of them may have been relieved in that way. Such an occurrence as that is very common where a surprise is attempted. In saying this, I don't wish to screen our officers from blame for some of them and some of the men are greatly to blame. In the first place, let us blame the department commander for stationing such a small number of troops at a post which is more exposed and easier surprised than any other in West Virginia. Secondly, I blame the post commandant (Col. Youart) for being very lenient in regard to picket and patrol duty. Those who succeeded in getting out of their quarters fought well as could be expected of men under the circumstances. Had they not made a charge and drove the Rebels some distance, I would have been eating horse meat in a Southern prison instead of writing this to you. But immediately after I was released, the Rebels were reenforced and came thundering down upon us taking all prisoners who were not pretty fleet footed.

I believe I told you in my last letter I was clerking in the Q.M. Dept. I am still clerking in it and am still boarding at a private residence.

I did lose my Housewife and would be very glad to receive another. You can send it by mail as safe as any other way. You can send anything less than four pounds. It is perfectly safe and costs but little.

Philippi, West Virginia
February 21, 1865

Congratulate me on my good fortune. I have a furlough for 20 days, but I have decided not to start home for a few days yet as the Q.M. wishes me to make up his returns for January. They are already nearly completed so that it will only cause a delay of three or four days. By that means, I will get my time lengthened for 25 days.

Please tell father that unless I get paid off before starting home (which I think not at all probable) I will want to get some money from him if he can spare it conveniently.

Philippi, West Virginia
March 20, 1865

I have the pleasure of announcing my safe arrival today

at noon. I stayed at Columbus Friday night and laid over at Bellaire 22 hours on account of missing connection. On arriving at the Ohio River, I found everything afloat. All of the houses in the lower part of town were submerged, some of them up to the second story. At one place, the railroad was covered with water to the depth of a foot for a half mile. The bridge across the Monongahela River on the Baltimore and Ohio Railroad was swept away, and we had to cross on ferry. Met a train on opposite side waiting for us so that we were only detained for a short time.

I arrived at Webster last evening and walked here today (12 miles), found the regiment in good spirits and everything lively.

There is a regiment of infantry at Beverly, and it is not improbable that we will be moved there soon as the roads improve.

Since arriving at the regiment, I feel as though I have just awoke from a pleasant dream of home and friends to find that I am still a soldier. However, I believe I am just as well contented as I would be at home. All that I have to regret is that I am spending several years of the most important time of my life in a way that will be of very little use to me when the war is over. It will take a great deal of close application and patient endurance to make up for lost time.

Would you believe it? The first greetings I received here were "congratulations" and best wishes for myself and **wife!** Some lady had written to Ed. Tomlinson that I was married but did not say to whom. Some of the boys still contend that I am joking when I deny it.

I suppose ere you answer this you will have the concert at Gettysburg. Please let me know how it goes off. Doubtless you will have a grand time.

I expect to stay here for awhile yet but have not determined what I will do.

Philippi, West Virginia
March 26, 1865

I am still here waiting orders. Spoke to Major Dotze this morning about going to Weston but was told to take it easy for awhile yet and probably he would have something for me to do. The regiment has built a summer residence on the opposite side *of the river and are moving today. They have heretofore occupied houses in town. They have very good quarters now built of logs and boards. This looks like staying here some time yet.*

I am under many obligations to you for those cigars you gave me. They are excellent. Better than we can get here for 5¢ each. I only smoke about one-third as much here as I did while at home. I think it is injurious to my health as well as pocket to smoke so much.

I purchased Moore's Poetical Works at Columbus and have read them nearly through. Will send them home soon as I finish and would advise you to peruse them. I have heretofore read a great many novels but have concluded to turn my attention for awhile at least to something more substantial.

Major Shaw is not able to take command of the regiment yet. Is president of a general court martial at Clarksburg.

A citizen of this place who has been in the rebel army came home today. He was in Early's Army, deserted from a hospital near Richmond, gave himself up to General Sheridan, took the oath, left him at the White House and arrived here today. He is a pitiable looking object. Says he was half starved until he reached our lines. Says he has not been paid for 18 months nor did he care to be paid for it would not have purchased half that many good meals. His wages was $18.00 per month. He says there is no hope for the South and that every southern soldier knows it.

We have had pretty rough weather since my arrival here. Snow most of the time.

There is intense excitement here in regard to a draft that took place two days ago. They drafted from an enrollment which took place more than two years ago which made it very heavy. Men were drafted who have been in the Rebel service two years and others who have been dead that length of time. The proportion is about one out of three, but it was their own fault for not having the enrollment attended to properly and of course they dare not resist while under the immediate rule of Federal bayonets. We are greeted by long faces on every side.

Weston, West Virginia
April 8, 1865

We have had a regular jubilee all day and this evening over the capture of General Lee and his army. I was drilling the company in the sabre exercise this morning when the dispatch came announcing the glorious news. Need I say we waved our sabres and hats and gave three long and loud cheers for the success of our arms.

I can find neither words or actions to express the unbounded joy I feel when I think over the many dangers and privations I have endured in the last four years with the rest of my comrades and that our earnest wish and that for which we have been fighting is nearly consummated.

We were called out this evening in front of the court house where we heard several excellent speeches accompanied by the stirring music of our regimental band. Cheer after cheer followed each other in rapid succession until the very mountains seemed alive with echoes. In the absence of artillery the men procured two anvils and up to this time have used about 16 lbs. of powder with no sign of cessation at least until the appearance of the small hours.

I arrived here from Philippi yesterday and this afternoon I received a detail in the Q.M. department. Have a very good position but plenty to do as I have a general supervision over all Q Master and commissary stores shipped to this place.

Weston, West Virginia
April 18, 1865

What a change has occurred since the date of my last letter. In the midst of such rejoicing as has never been equaled in the United States we receive the sad news that one who we had almost begun to idolize has been assassinated, murdered and our national colors have been wrapped in the sable hues of mourning.

Tomorrow all business is to be suspended and 21 guns will be fired at 12:40.

I am still in the Q.M. and doing very well.

Weston, West Virginia
April 27, 1865

I wish you had been a little more explicit in your account of the exultation of the Butternuts over Lincoln's assassination. John Drischman's wife wrote that the Butternut Layers tied hemp on their doorknobs. I cannot believe that would have been allowed but if they showed any signs of exultation at all *they should have been made to suffer for it.*

Paroled men from the Army of Northern Virginia are reporting here daily in squads. One captain and several men live in the town and vicinity. They have been fighting us for four years and one month ago would have delighted in murdering everyone of us and pillaging the country. But now since their cause is hopeless they claim the same protection from the very Government they have fought, with a desperation worthy of a better cause, to destroy, that will be granted to us when we are discharged from the service. One fellow came in last evening who belonged to McCausland's command and fought us on our way to Lynchburg and again in the Valley, had fought against our regiment more than a dozen times and assisted in burning Chambersburg. Yet with all that I could not triumph over a fallen foe but gave him rations and lodging notwithstanding had I listened to the dictates of conscience, I would rather have seen him sentenced to the Dry Tortugas for life. I told him this and he said if the U.S. Government would banish every one of them he could but acknowledge the justice of the act and was willing to go at any time. However, I would not advocate such a measure as I want to see the difficulties adjusted peaceably as possible, to be permanent. I think secession has received a blow from which it will never recover in this continent and it only remains to restore peace and quietude throughout the land on the best possible terms.

I received a paper from Frank Howendobler some time ago from which it seems that he is one of the publishers while Arvin is proprietor of a drug store. They must have come out very fast since they left Hillgrove.

By the way I must not forget to tell you that I have started a cigar factory. I furnish the tobacco and David Keel makes it up on the halves. We have no revenue to pay so that we make about $1.00 or a little over per 100. He makes about one hundred per day besides doing his duty. When we get the thing under good headway he will make more than that per day.

John Barrack arrived here this evening but I have not seen him yet.

Weston, West Virginia
May 8, 1865

All the men of Co. G were today sent to Clarksburg on

detail in the Q.M. department. All the citizens who were employed as teamsters & c. were discharged and their places are to be filled by soldiers. This is the first act of entrenchment by the Government. There is to be a very heavy sale of Government property at that place on the 20th or 25th of this month. The sale will consist of horses, mules, harness, wagons, and in short Government property of most every kind. If it were not so far I would advise father, if he had a few hundred dollars to invest to attend it. But I suppose it is too far from home. I expect some of the property will go very cheap.

The citizens of this place met today and passed resolutions not to let any of the Rebs who lived in the county previous to enlisting in the Rebel army come to their homes. The resolutions were passed unanimously. I suppose no one will deny the justice of the act but I fear it will cause some trouble. Quite a number have returned already and are ordered to leave.

Now I will tell you my first experience in society at Weston. I received an invitation to attend a surprise party to be held last Friday evening about two miles in the country. The conveyances were as follows: one stage, one spring wagon and one buggy, all the vehicles that could be procured in the town. Capt. Criswell of the 17th Va. Inf. and I took the spring wagon and started for some of the fair sex. He was acquainted with them but I was not.

We got five ladies and started for the party in high glee but had not got out of town when the lines broke and the horse came very near running off. The ladies refused to go any further in the wagon so we were obliged to retrace our steps to the residence of one of the ladies and send for the stage to make a second trip, which done we arrived at our destination about 9 p.m., fashionable hours, found quite a large and interesting party of about 30 ladies and 15 gentlemen. The gentlemen consisted of 5 citizens and all the rest were officers except myself.

There was but one lady present that I was acquainted with but I had introductions to the rest and was soon in the height of my enjoyment. I was surprised to find the degree of intelligence and refinement that was there. I think I never saw a more sociable and refined circle of society. We had two large parlors in one of which was a pianoforte while in the other was card tables, chess, backgammon, dominoes and a game

Party at a Private Home, Weston, West Virginia, May 1865.

called authors. The last I never saw played before but it is a truly interesting game. It is played with cards made for the purpose and can be participated in by 12 players or less. We also played charades awhile. Time passed by pleasantly until 2 o'clock when the first stage load went home but as we had to wait for the second train we had daylight to go home by.

Last evening while walking the streets I was hailed with the salutation "Philaphoena" acknowledged beat and accompanied the two ladies home, passed an hour or so (probably so) very pleasantly and returned to the office with three novels to read. During the conversation one of the ladies challenged me for a horseback ride today but the rain has been descending in torrents all day so that we were disappointed. She also gave me an invitation to bring some of my comrades with their ladies this evening and we would have a parlour dance but in this we were also disappointed from the same cause, however there is a ball in town this evening which I will attend soon as I finish this letter but with no intention to participate as it is a miscellaneous gathering.

Weston next to Hagerstown is the gayest place I have seen outside of Ohio.

Several members of the Detachment at Weston returned to that community after the war and became founders of well-known local families.[4]

Weston, West Virginia
May 19, 1865

Please tell father I would like to have $10.00 **soon as I can get it if convenient.** We have no news of the paymaster yet. Will not probably be paid until discharged.

The regiment is to be concentrated here. Late Captain Owens of the regular army is our colonel. He is very strict. Have no idea how soon we will be mustered out but not for one or two months yet.

Clarksburg, West Virginia
May 30, 1865

The regiment is paid off and I sent father $525 by express. You will find the receipts enclosed. I received 13 months' pay ($398.00) including $150.00 bounty. The men of 1862, S. Myers,

John Barrack, the Bierly boys and others, 16 in all, were discharged from the service today. They start for Columbus tomorrow. Will remain there several days to get paid. Will probably be home Saturday.

It was the prevailing opinion in the regiment that we would go to Texas until today. We hear that Smith has surrendered. If this be true I think we will be discharged within a few months although I hardly expect it very soon as Gov. Brough has made a special request to the War Department that we be retained as the last Ohio regiment to be discharged. I want you to do all you can for him if he runs for governor this fall. I would almost as soon vote for a butternut as for him.

Our colonel gets along with the men better than he did at first. We begin to like him pretty well. I am kept very busy now making out accounts for officers. They all want to get square before we are discharged.

Clarksburg, West Virginia
June 14, 1865

I promised to write to you from Beverly but we were only there a few days and my mind was so fully occupied that I neglected to fulfill my promise. We went as far as that place with the regiment and remained there while the regiment went on a scout to the vicinity of Warm Springs and then accompanied them in their return to this place.

There is still a great diversity of opinion as to how soon we will be discharged from the service. Some of the knowing ones predict that we will go to Kentucky or Missouri while others persist in the opinion that we will be discharged soon. I understand there is an order to muster out all men who have been prisoners. If so, our regiment will be almost broken up. It will leave only about 6 or 8 of us veterans of our company with about 30 recruits. There is a strong desire throughout the regiment to retire from service and I cannot think the Government will retain volunteers who want to retire from the service any longer than is absolutely necessary. But it will require several months yet to muster them all out. I suppose our men of 1862 are enjoying the pleasure of civilized life by this time. I wish that I could say as much. Soldiers are passing here at the rate of about 100 car loads per day.

I forgot to mention the object of the raid and doubtless you wonder what its purpose was. They intended to endeavor to capture Extra Billy Smith and several other ex Rebel officials but they were captured before our regiment arrived. They then turned their attention to collecting Government horses and other property which had been abandoned in that country, but in short the expedition amounted to almost nothing.

Did father receive the money I sent him? Please write soon and send two of my photographs if you have them to spare. I forget whether I have any at home or not.

I send you a Rebel flag which was made by a Miss Campbell of Philippi in 1861 and kept by her until this week. She gave it to me saying the war was over and she would surrender formally and become as enthusiastic in favor of the U.S. Government as she was in the southern cause. She was arrested several times for expressing disloyal sentiments and always kept this and another flag concealed while our troops held the place. You will notice the flag only bears one star. It is a Virginia flag and was made before they knew how many states were to be represented.

At Beverly and Philippi and in fact through all that part of the country nearly every other man one sees is a returned Rebel. They seem completely subdued and anxious as ever to only be let alone. The Union people in their intercourse with them usually show them the cold shoulder, however, I attended a party at a Rebel major's house in Philippi last week where every thing passed off harmoniously. At Beverly the Rebels had a dance but did not invite any Union soldiers and but few Union citizens. However, the country will have to be strongly garrisoned for some time yet as there are a great many old feuds to settle up between the two parties.

Clarksburg, West Virginia
June 25, 1865

I received a letter from father dated June 15th acknowledging receipt of money &c. It is now pretty definitely ascertained that we will remain here until discharged. As to how soon that will be we have no knowledge but it will not be for awhile yet, although I think the veterans will have a chance soon as circumstances will permit.

The surrender of Miss Campbell of Philippi, West Virginia

Preparation for celebrating the 4th is the all absorbing theme of conversation here. Our regiment has three invitations, one here, one at Weston and one about five miles in the country. They will all be represented as we will probably be allowed to go to any of them we wish to.

The opinion of the regiment is changing very rapidly in favor of our Colonel. He is the kindest hearted man we ever had to command us, has never refused a favor to any of the regiment when he could possibly grant it. There was a very strong prejudice against him before he came to us but that is rapidly subsiding.

I subscribed for an illustrated paper for Jennie. It is a newspaper just started by Frank Leslie in New York and is called "The Chimney Corner." I subscribed for 13 weeks to try it. She will get one this week. I have also subscribed for it myself or rather two of us have in partnership.

Clarksburg, West Virginia
July 2, 1865

There has been some excitement in the regiment for the last week in regard to our muster out of service. Papers have been eagerly scanned in the vain endeavor to find an order that would include us but as yet our efforts have been fruitless although I think the authorities are beginning to see the matter in the proper light and will muster the veteran regiments out soon as practicable.

Six companies of the regiment received orders yesterday for a ten days' scout. The order was obeyed very reluctantly this morning as the men had made sure of a grand time on the 4th. Several companies refused to go at first and only responded to "Boots and Saddle" after a great deal of argument and I may say coaxing as it is too late to use threats. You have no idea of the state of feeling in the army for the papers studiously avoid publishing accounts of mutinies and refusals to obey orders that occur daily. Yesterday our regiment and the 74th Pa. Infantry were called out to arrest a New York regiment that, becoming indignant at the idea of being sent west, became lawless and unmanageable. They were prevailed on to take the cars at Washington but commenced to pillage houses and get drunk at every station where they stopped. However the matter was deferred until their arrival at Parkersburg where they were to be arrested by two other regiments but I doubt whether any men can be prevailed upon to arrest them. I am confident our regiment and the 74th could not have been. The New York regiment were veterans and were very indignant at being sent west when western nonveterans were being mustered out.

I had quite a lengthy ride on horseback with a lady of Clarksburg today. We went 12 miles and back, 24 miles in all, from 10 a.m. til 2 p.m. Pretty good time wasn't it? There were four of us in the party. We had a very pleasant time but the excursion was a little too lengthy and we were somewhat fatigued on our return. 24 miles is a long distance to ride without being out of the saddle.

It is surprising what equestrians these Virginia ladies are. They never seem to tire of riding horseback. One lady has attracted considerable attention from the regiment. She rides out every evening unattended by anyone and may be seen just before dusk each evening riding past camp at full speed. If she wishes to get off in town to do some shopping she jumps off the horse on to the ground without any aid and having finished shopping places her hands on the horse's neck and the saddle and with a bound is seated in the saddle and the next instant is seen disappearing at full speed. She is known only as the butcher's daughter. I have heard her name but forget it. On arriving home from her excursions she raises up in her saddle, vaults gracefully over the fence into the yard and with a cut from her whip sends her horse to the stable. Her father is wealthy having amassed a fortune by furnishing beef for the army.

Do you know where Samuel Stahl is? He is reported by the company as "Paroled Prisoner of War at Camp Chase, Ohio" but I think he has deserted. He has some $350 due him which can be collected and he can get an honorable discharge if he will report to Camp Chase and send an application here for his descriptive roll approved by the General commanding. I send a form for application which please give him if he is at home as I would not like to see him lose his money which he will do if it is found out he is not at Camp Chase when he will be reported a deserter and under recent orders will lose all pay and bounty. In case he goes to Camp Chase all he has to do is give this application to W.A. McGrew, A.A.G. Camp

Chase, Ohio who will send it here, obtain his descriptive list and have him mustered out and paid off in full. (Fill out the date.) Ben Hurley has deserted, would have received about $280 if he had remained until we were mustered out. The orders are to report anyone who is absent from his command 24 hours as a deserter when they are to be dropped from the rolls and will not collect their dues. Hurley could collect his money if he would return soon as he has not been reported as a deserter yet, hoping he would return.

Clarksburg, West Virginia
July 10, 1865

I hardly know what reply to make to your inquiry as to what profession or business I will adopt when I get home. I have not as yet given up the idea of a mercantile life although I have thought seriously of late that I could perhaps do better at something else. But what shall that something else be? I must confess that I am at a loss to know. My only objection to taking a mercantile course is that there are a great many men in the army who have held clerkships until they have obtained a pretty good use of the pen and now nine-tenths of them intend to adopt that profession thus rendering it an asylum for a lot of men who are too lazy to do anything else. If I had the necessary capital to start on I would not give it up as I believe I am better fitted for that than anything else. Of the professions, I have thought that of medicine would be preferable however I will not decide until I get home and look around awhile first. Tenacity of purpose is so much a part of my nature that I will only give up a resolution I have adhered to so long after mature consideration.

We intended having a grand celebration here on the 4th but failed most ignominiously. There was $200 raised in the regiment besides that contributed by the citizens. The procession consisted of about 100 soldiers and not a citizen but the dinner beggared description. It consisted of Government bread and beef and a few chickens and sole leather pies. After helping a couple of ladies to a bit of chicken and pie I found that everything had disappeared so I went to a Catholic fair which was held in an adjacent grove and purchased a passable dinner. They were having a lively time dancing & c. so I passed the afternoon with them. The other celebration, in fact both of *them, were got up by citizens.*

There is a prospect of getting mustered out in about a month. Most of the men are out on a scout beyond Beverly and will not return until about the 15th.

Has Jennie received her paper yet? I received all the back numbers (6 in number) and like it very well.

Clarksburg, West Virginia
July 19, 1865

Doubtless you are expecting to see us home every day but you will have to look for some time yet. It is a huge task to muster out a regiment and especially a cavalry regiment. To muster out our regiment it would take 15 clerks 5 days to only make out the necessary papers. Each company is required to make out 7 muster and pay rolls each of which would cover a good sized table. Our roll has 136 men on it and we have to give each man's rank, age, time and place of enlistment and by whom enlisted, period enlisted for, and by whom, mustered into service to what time and by whom paid, amount of bounty due and received and also account for every man who has ever belonged to the company whether discharged, died, deserted or transferred. Then each man's discharge is to write out on parchment rolls separate; each man's clothing is to be computed from January 1, 1865. All clothing accounts were captured at Beverly so we count it square up to that time. Since that, our clothing allowance in money is $43 of which I have drawn $19 in clothing leaving a balance due me on clothing of $24 which will be given to me in addition to my pay. Most of the men have drawn clothing during the same time to the amount of from $45 to $70. One man high as $101 so he will owe the Government $58 to be stopped from his pay.

It is not known how soon we will leave for Cincinnati to be paid but think it will be before August 1st. We will have not turned over horses or other stores yet.

The regiment returned from the scout a few days ago. Made several important captures, viz. two pet bears, 3 pet foxes, besides several dogs, guinea pigs & c. We have quite a menagerie.

Horse racing is our favorite amusement and is participated in by nearly every man in the regiment. Every evening

Return of the regiment with important captures, July 1865

bets are frequently made from $5 to $50. I have the fastest horse in the company but have never bet on him. Beat the captain's horse this evening. Could have had a bet to any amount.

Apparently the sport of horse racing continued in spite of General Order No. 7 issued by the regimental commander, Lt. Colonel Augustus Dotze. The order dated June 28, 1865, stated:
"The attention of the company commanders is called to the unnecessary running of horses and fast riding by enlisted men; this must not be tolerated: Officers have been reminded of this miserable practice so frequently and all know the evil growing out of it."[5]

Clarksburg, West Virginia
July 21, 1865
I received your letter containing $10 yesterday and am truly thankful for it. I was not quite out yet but was closer run than I wished to be while en route for Camp Dennison. We will start for that place about next Wednesday or Thursday.

The men of the 8th Ohio were mustered out of service on July 30, 1865, at Clarksburg, West Virginia.

Cincinnati, Ohio
August 3, 1865
We arrived here this morning. The regiment goes to Camp Dennison today but I will remain in the city until tomorrow. Would like to see you down if you can spare the time. It would be a pleasant visit. We will remain at Camp D. until next Monday or perhaps a few days later.

Epilogue

"Died — McKee

At his father's residence in Union City, Indiana, on Tuesday, March 6, 1877, of consumption. John A. McKee, aged 34 years."

Miami Democrat,
Piqua, Ohio
March 17, 1877

John was buried in the Gettysburg, Ohio, Cemetery. His mother, Sarah Jane Harper McKee, had been buried there some 10 years earlier after giving birth to her 11th child. Two siblings, Susan and Elizabeth who had died young, were also there. Later, John's brother William who died in 1905 and sister Margaret (Maggie) (1943) were added to the family plot. John's government headstone carries an erroneous date of his death as January 9, 1903. In researching names of deceased Civil War veterans, another J.A. McKee was apparently deemed to be buried there. Family records agree with the above newspaper account.

John's father, Washington Joseph McKee, remarried in 1873 to Lemira Elliott Coots and moved to Union City, Ohio, a community on the Indiana boundary where he operated a grocery store. He also served as a public official. Following John's death and in 1878 Mr. McKee moved his family to a farm in Kansas located southeast of Topeka near Richland.

James T. McKee, to whom most of John's letters were written, became a proprietor of a bookstore in Clinton, Missouri. He married Mary Frances Rickets in 1873. She died in 1895; James in 1909.

NOTES

1861
1. *Springfield Republic*, Monday, October 7, 1861, Ohio Historical Society.
2. Foote, Shelby, The Civil War. A Narrative, Vol. I, pp. 69-70.
3. Coles, Harry L., Ohio Forms an Army, p. 22, 1962.
4. Official Records of the War of the Rebellion, Series I, Vol. V, p. 377.
5. *Springfield Republic*, Monday, November 25, 1861, Ohio Historical Society.
6. Stutler, Boyd B., West Virginia in the Civil War, 1963m Education Foundation, Inc., Charleston, W. Va.
7. *Springfield Republic*, Friday, December 6, 1861, Ohio Historical Society.
8. Regimental papers, National Archives, Washington, D.C.

1862
1. National Archives, Washington, D.C.
2. Official Roster, Soldiers of the State of Ohio, Vol. XI, p. 432.
3. Special Order No. 21, Regimental Order and Guard Report Book, National Archives, Washington, D.C.
4. Regimental Papers, National Archives.
5. Stutler
6. Cox, Jacob Dolson, Military Reminiscences of the War, Vol. I, p. 158, 1900.
7. Regimental papers, National Archives, Washington, D.C.
8. Reid, Whitelaw, Ohio in the War: Her Statesmen, Her Generals and Soldiers, p. 278; Boatner, Mark M. III, The Civil War Dictionary, pp. 908, 909.
9. *Springfield Republic*, September 19, 1862. Ohio Historical Society.
10. Special Order no. 58, Department of the Ohio, Regimental Papers, National Archives, Washington, D.C.
11. Harrison, Lowell H., The Civil War in Kentucky, pp. 4 et seq.
12. Johnson, Rossiter, Campfires and Battlefields, p. 41.
13. Butler, Lorine Letcher, John Morgan and His Men, 1960, pp. 193 et seq.

1863
1. *Tri-Weekly Commonwealth*, Frankfort, Ky., February 19, 1863.
2. *Tri-Weekly Commonwealth*, Frankfort, Ky., February 19, 1863.
3. Coulter, E. Merton, The Civil War and Readjustment in Kentucky, pp. 170 et seq.
4. Reid, Whitelaw, Ohio in the War: Her Generals and Soldiers, Vol. I.
5. Official Reports of the War of the Rebellion, Series I, Vol. XXIII, Pt.

1, pp. 384-389. Foote, Shelby, The Civil War, a Narrative, Vol. 2, p. 677, Seymour, kDigby Gordon, Divided Loyalties, pp. 74 et seq.

1864

1. Reid, Whitelaw, "Ohio in the War: Her Statesmen, Her Generals and Soldiers," 1868, p. 279.
2. Regimental Records, National Archives, Washington, D.C.
3. Special Order No. 8, Regimental Records, National Archives, Washington, D.C.
4. *The Springfield Republic,* February 1, 1864.
5. *The Springfield Republic,* March 23, 1864.
6. Pamphlet, Cincinnati Public Library.
7. *The Springfield Republic,* April 25, 1864.
8. The Crisis, April 27, 1864.
9. O.R. Vol. XXXVII, Series 1.p. 145
10. For Confederate General John A. Imboden's statement regarding the trial and execution of David S. Creigh see Rossiter John's Campfires and Battlefields, pp. 317, 318. See also "David S. Creigh — Greenbrier Martyr" by Shirley Donelly, D.D., West Virginia Historical Society. (1950).
11. Clark County Historical Society records, Springfield, Ohio.
12. Ohio State Historical Society, Columbus, Ohio.
13. Catton, Bruce, Grant Takes Command, pp. 298 35 seq.
14. Early, Jubal Anderson, Autobiographical Sketch and Narrative of the War Between the States, pp. 375, 379.
15. *The Springfield Republic,* July 8, 1864.
16. Official Roster of the Soldiers of the State of Ohio in the War of the Rebellion, Vol. XI, p. 401.
17. National Archives, Washington, D.C.
18. Reid, Whitelaw, Ohio in the War: Her Statesmen, Her Generals and Soldiers, Vol. II, p. 806.
19. National Archives, Washington, D.C.

1865

1. Official Records of the War of the Rebellion, Series I, Vol. LXVI, pp. 447 et seq.
2. O.R. Series I, Vol. LXVI, p. 449.
3. Reid, Whitelaw, Ohio in the War: Her Statesmen, Her Generals and Soldiers, p. 403, 1868.
4. Cook, Roy Bird, Lewis County in the Civil War, 1924. West Virginia Historical Society.
5. General Order No. 7, Clarksburg, West Virginia, June 28, 1865. Regimental papers, National Archives, Washington, D.C.

APPENDIX

OFFICIAL ROSTER
of the
SOLDIERS OF THE STATE OF OHIO
of the
WAR OF THE REBELLION
1861-1865
Vols. IV and XI

44th REGIMENT OHIO VOLUNTEER INFANTRY

Field and Staff

Mustered in Oct. 14, 1861, at Camp Clark, Ohio, by J.H. Young, Captain 15th Infantry, U.S.A. Consolidated with 8th Ohio Volunteer Cavalry, Jan. 4, 1864, at Cincinnati, Ohio.

Names	Rank	Age	Date of Entering the Service	Period of Service
Samuel A. Gilbert	Colonel	-	Oct. 14, 1861	3 yrs.
Transferred to 8th O.V.C. Jan. 4, 1864				
H. Blair Wilson	Lt. Col.	34	Sept. 5, 1861	3 yrs.
Resigned April 9, 1863				
Lysander W. Tulleys	Lt. Col.	26	Sept. 5, 1861	3 yrs.
Promoted from Captain Co. D, April 9, 1863; discharged Jan. 30, 1864				
Ackber O. Mitchell	Major	28	Oct. 8, 1861	3 yrs.
Resigned June 5, 1863				
Alpheus S. Moore	Major	23	Aug. 31, 1861	3 yrs.
Promoted from Captain Co. A, April 19, 1863; transferred to 8th O.V.C. Jan. 4, 1864				
Henry K. Steele	Surgeon	36	Sept. 26, 1861	3 yrs.
Transferred to 8th O.V.C. Jan. 4, 1864				
John H. Rodgers	As. Surg.	27	Sept. 26, 1861	3 yrs.
Promoted to Surgeon 104th O.V.I. Feb. 14, 1863				
Douglass Luce	As. Surg.	-	July 4, 1863	3 yrs.
Discharged Jan. 30, 1864				
Benjamin F. Davis	As. Surg.	-	March 11, 1863	3 yrs.
Transferred to 8th O.V.C., Jan 4, 1864				
John G. Telford	Adjutant	18	Aug. 20, 1861	3 yrs.
Promoted from Sergeant Co. A. Aug. 22, 1861; transferred to 8th O.V.C. Jan. 4, 1864				
Jeremiah Klinefelter	R.Q.M.	41	Sept. 24, 1861	3 yrs.
Killed Aug. 7, 1862, in action at Meadow Bluff, West Virginia				
Thomas B. Douglass	R.Q.M.	31	Sept. 20, 1861	3 yrs.
Promoted from 2d Lieutenant Co. A, Aug. 7, 1862				
Thomas P. Childs	Chaplain	44	Oct. 10, 1861	3 yrs.
Discharged Nov. 6, 1862				
Lafayett Bechtol	Ser. Maj.	21	Sept. 16, 1861	3 yrs.
Promoted from Sergeant Co. I, Oct. 9, 1861; transferred to 8th O.V.C. Jan. 4, 1864; veteran				
Joseph McIntyre	Com. Ser.	45	Sept. 14, 1861	3 yrs.
Promoted from private Co. F, Sept. 14, 1861; mustered out Jan. 20, 1864, at Cincinnati, O., by order of War Department				

44th REGIMENT OHIO VOLUNTEER INFANTRY *(Continued)*

Names	Rank	Age	Date of Entering the Service	Period of Service
John B. Fagan	Q.M. Ser.	37	Sept. 16, 1861	3 yrs.

Promoted from private Co. E, Sept. 16, 1861; transferred to 8th O.V.C. Jan. 4, 1864; veteran

Silas, Edgar F.	Hos. St'd	28	Oct. 10, 1861	3 yrs.

Promoted from private Co. K, Oct. 10, 1861; transferred to 8th O.V.C. Jan. 4, 1864; veteran

Company G.

Mustered in Sept. 23, 1861, at Camp Clark, Ohio, by J.H. Young, Captain 15th Infantry, U.S.A. Consolidated with Co. G, 8th Ohio Volunteer Cavalry, Jan. 4, 1864, at Cincinnati, Ohio.

John M. Newkirk	Captain	31	Sept. 20, 1861	3 yrs.

Resigned May 29, 1863

James W. Shaw	Captain	22	Sept. 20, 1861	3 yrs.

Promoted from 1st Lieutenant May 29, 1863; transferred to Co. G, 8th O.V.C. Jan. 4, 1864

Anson N. Thompson	1st Lieut.	22	Sept. 5, 1861	3 yrs.

Promoted to 2d Lieutenant from 1st Sergeant Co. C, March 31, 1861; 1st Lieutenant, May 29, 1863; transferred to Co. B, 8th O.V.C. Jan. 4, 1864

Samuel Judy	2d Lieut.	24	Sept. 20, 1861	3 yrs.

Resigned March 31, 1862

Alexander McAlpine	2d Lieut.	32	Sept. 20, 1861	3 yrs.

Promoted from 1st Sergeant, May 29, 1863; transferred to Co. G, 8th O.V.C., Jan. 4, 1864

William H. Tate	1st Sergt.	21	Sept. 20, 1861	3 yrs.

Appointed from Sergeant —; transferred to Co. G, 8th O.V.C., Jan. 4, 1864

David N. Craig	Sergeant	19	Sept. 20, 1861	3 yrs.

Appointed from Corporal —; transferred to Co. G, 8th O.V.C., Jan. 4, 1864

William H. Creeger	Sergeant	19	Sept. 20, 1861	3 yrs.

Transferred to Co. G, 8th O.V.C., Jan 4, 1864; veteran

William E. Kerlinger	Sergeant	26	Sept. 20, 1861	3 yrs.

Appointed from private —; transferred to Co. G, 8th O.V.C., Jan. 4, 1864; veteran

Frank E. Moores	Sergeant	20	Sept. 20, 1861	3 yrs.

Promoted to 2d Lieutenant Co. D, Oct. 5, 1862

44th REGIMENT OHIO VOLUNTEER INFANTRY *(Continued)*

Names	Rank	Age	Date of Entering the Service	Period of Service
George H. Potter	Sergeant	21	Sept. 20, 1861	

Transferred to Co. G, 8th O.V.C., Jan 4, 1864

Benjamin Adams	Corporal	25	Sept. 20, 1861	3 yrs.

Transferred to Co. G, 8th O.V.C., Jan. 4, 1864

John Cartner	Corporal	21	Sept. 20, 1861	3 yrs.

Appointed Corporal —; transferred to Co. G, 8th O.V.C., Jan. 4, 1864; veteran

John H. Friday	Corporal	19	Sept. 20, 1861	3 yrs.

Appointed Corporal —; transferred to Co. G, 8th O.V.C., Jan. 4, 1864; veteran

William B. Galloway	Corporal	20	Sept. 20, 1861	3 yrs.

Transferred to Co. G, 8th O.V.C., Jan. 4, 1864; veteran

John E. Harrison	Corporal	21	Sept. 20, 1861	3 yrs.

Transferred to Co. G, 8th O.V.C., Jan. 4, 1864; veteran

Samuel J. Harrison	Corporal	22	Sept. 20, 1861	3 yrs.

Appointed Corporal —; transferred to Co. G, 8th O.V.C., Jan. 4, 1864; veteran

William Hayes	Corporal	43	Sept. 20, 1861	3 yrs.

Discharged Oct. 14, 1862, at Gallipolis, O., on Surgeon's certificate of disability

Rufus Kent	Corporal	34	Sept. 20, 1861	3 yrs.

Appointed Corporal —; transferred to Co. G, 8th O.V.C., Jan. 4, 1864; veteran

John A. McKee	Corporal	19	Sept. 20, 1861	3 yrs.

Transferred to Co. G, 8th O.V.C., Jan. 4, 1864; veteran

William A. Martin	Corporal	20	Sept. 20, 1861	3 yrs.

Transferred to Co. G, 8th O.V.C., Jan. 4, 1864; veteran

Samuel F. Reed	Corporal	26	Sept. 20, 1861	3 yrs.

Transferred to Co. G, 8th O.V.C., Jan. 4, 1864; veteran

William H. Robbins	Corporal	25	Sept. 20, 1861	3 yrs.

Appointed Corporal —; transferred to Co. G, 8th O.V.C., Jan. 4, 1864; veteran

James Dunham	Musician	41	Sept. 20, 1861	3 yrs.

Discharged Dec. 27, 1862, at Columbus, O., on Surgeon's certificate of disability

Charles D. Felton	Musician	39	Sept. 20, 1861	3 yrs.

Discharged Jan. 25, 1863, at Frankfort, Ky., on Surgeon's certificate of disability

Edward Bond	Wagoner	32	Sept. 20, 1861	3 yrs

Discharged Jan. 8, 1863, at Lexington, Ky., on Surgeon's certificate of

44th REGIMENT OHIO VOLUNTEER INFANTRY *(Continued)*

Names	Rank	Age	Date of Entering the Service	Period of Service

disability

Alred, Emerson .... Private   24   Sept. 20, 1861   3 yrs.
    Died Jan. 31, 1862, at Camp Piatt, W. Va.

Alspaugh, Henry .... Private   31   Sept. 20, 1861   3 yrs.
    Discharged to date, Aug. 31, 1862, on Surgeon's certificate of disability

Anderson, Charles .... Private   18   Sept. 20, 1861   3 yrs.
    Discharged Oct. 16, 1862, at Gallipolis, O., on Surgeon's certificate of disability

Arens, Granville M. .... Private   19   Sept. 20, 1861   3 yrs.
    Transferred to Co. G, 8th O.V.C., Jan. 4, 1864; veteran

Barnhart, James W. .... Private   19   Sept. 19, 1861   3 yrs.
    Transferred to Mississippi Marine Brigade, April 4, 1863

Bennett, Samuel .... Private   19   Sept. 19, 1861   3 yrs.
    Transferred to Co. G, 8th O.V.C., Jan. 4, 1864; veteran

Benson, Elijah M. .... Private   21   Sept. 19, 1861   3 yrs.
    Transferred to Co. G, 8th O.V.C., Jan. 4, 1864

Bishop, Samuel .... Private   18   Sept. 19, 1861   3 yrs.
    Transferred to Co. G, 8th O.V.C., Jan. 4, 1864; veteran

Brown, Jacob B. .... Private   27   Sept. 29, 1861   3 yrs.
    Transferred to Co. G, 8th O.V.C., Jan. 4, 1864; veteran

Byers, Alanson .... Private   19   Sept. 19, 1861   3 yrs.
    Transferred to Co. G, 8th O.V.C., Jan. 4, 1864; veteran

Byers, Harvey A. .... Private   21   Sept. 19, 1861   3 yrs.
    Transferred to Co., G, 8th O.V.C., Jan. 4, 1864; veteran

Clark, Thomas M. .... Private   21   Sept. 20, 1861   3 yrs.
    Transferred to Co. G, 8th O.V.C., Jan. 4, 1864; veteran

Conner, David O. .... Private   21   Sept. 20, 1861   3 yrs.
    Transferred to Co. G, 8th O.V.C., Jan. 4, 1864; veteran

Conner, William .... Private   19   Sept. 20, 1861   3 yrs.
    Transferred to Co. G, 8th O.V.C., Jan. 4, 1864; veteran

Corgin, Joseph H. .... Private   18   Sept. 20, 1861   3 yrs.
    Transferred to Co. G, 8th O.V.C., Jan. 4, 1864; veteran

Cox, William .... Private   23   Sept. 20, 1861   3 yrs.
    Died June 15, 1863, at Lexington, Ky.

Craig, Francis M. .... Private   18   Sept. 20, 1861   3 yrs.
    Transferred to Co. G, 8th O.V.C., Jan. 4, 1864; veteran

44th REGIMENT OHIO VOLUNTEER INFANTRY *(Continued)*

Names	Rank	Age	Date of Entering the Service	Period of Service
Deeds, William	Private	20	Sept. 20, 1861	3 yrs.
Transferred to Co. G, 8th O.V.C., Jan. 4, 1864; veteran				
Drew, James	Private	24	Sept. 20, 1861	3 yrs.
Discharged July 25, 1862, at Cincinnati, O., on Surgeon's certificate of disability				
Engle, Silas P.	Private	19	Sept. 20, 1861	3 yrs.
Transferred to Co. G, 8th O.V.C., Jan. 4, 1864; veteran				
Felton, Robert D.	Private	19	Sept. 20, 1861	3 yrs.
Transferred to Co. G, 8th O.V.C., Jan. 4, 1864; veteran				
Flemming, Charles	Private	21	Sept. 20, 1861	3 yrs.
Transferred to Co. G, 8th O.V.C., Jan. 4, 1864; veteran				
Foutz, Lewis	Private	32	Sept. 20, 1861	3 yrs.
Transferred from Co. C, Oct. 31, 1861; discharged Oct. 4, 1862, in General Hospital at Gallipolis, O., on Surgeon's certificate of disability				
Galloway, Joshua G.	Private	18	Sept. 20, 1861	3 yrs.
Transferred to Co. G, 8th O.V.C., Jan. 4, 1864; veteran				
Ganger, Wm. H.	Private	19	Sept. 20, 1861	3 yrs.
Transferred to Co. G, 8th O.V.C., Jan. 4, 1864; veteran				
Graham, John W.	Private	18	Sept. 20, 1861	3 yrs.
Transferred to Co. G, 8th O.V.C., Jan. 4, 1864; veteran				
Hall, Marquis L.	Private	26	Sept. 20, 1861	3 yrs.
Transferred to Co. G, 8th O.V.C., Jan. 4, 1864; veteran				
Harper, Benjamin	Private	27	Sept. 20, 1861	3 yrs.
Transferred to Co. G, 8th O.V.C., Jan. 4, 1864; veteran				
Harmon, Abram I.	Private	41	Sept. 20, 1861	3 yrs.
Died March 6, 1862, at Dallas, Highland County, O.				
Harrison, George W.	Private	19	Sept. 20, 1861	3 yrs.
Discharged Oct. 7, 1862, at Gallipolis, O., on Surgeon's certificate of disability				
Hurley, Benjamin	Private	19	Sept. 20, 1861	3 yrs.
Transferred to Co. G, 8th O.V.C., Jan. 4, 1864; veteran				
Johnson, Francis L.	Private	20	Sept. 20, 1861	3 yrs.
Transferred to Co. G, 8th O.V.C., Jan. 4, 1864; veteran				
Kesler, George	Private	19	Sept. 20, 1861	3 yrs.
Transferred to Co. G, 8th O.V.C., Jan. 4, 1864; veteran				
Kiefer, Christian	Private	26	Sept. 20, 1861	3 yrs.
Transferred to Co. G, 8th O.V.C., Jan. 4, 1864; veteran				
Long, George W.	Private	19	Sept. 20, 1861	3 yrs.
Died May 19, 1862, at Charleston, W. Va.				

44th REGIMENT OHIO VOLUNTEER INFANTRY *(Continued)*

Names	Rank	Age	Date of Entering the Service	Period of Service
McClenan, William D.	Private	18	Sept. 20, 1861	3 yrs.
McDonald, Mark	Private	19	Sept. 20, 1861	3 yrs.

Discharged Nov. 30, 1861, at Camp Piatt, W. Va., on Surgeon's certificate of disability

McQuay, Elias	Private	19	Sept. 20, 1861	3 yrs.

Discharged May 1, 1862, at Camp Piatt, W. Va., on Surgeon's certificate of disability

Meeker, Rufus G.	Private	19	Sept. 20, 1861	3 yrs.

Transferred to Co. G, 8th O.V.C., Jan. 4, 1864; veteran

Miller, Newton G.	Private	19	Sept. 20, 1861	3 yrs.

Died Oct. 22, 1862, at Greenville, Darke County, Ohio

Moter, Irvin	Private	31	Sept. 20, 1861	3 yrs.

Transferred to Co. G, 8th O.V.C., Jan. 4, 1864; veteran

Mullinex, Henry	Private	19	Sept. 20, 1861	3 yrs.

Discharged Jan. 10, 1862, at Camp Piatt, W. Va., on Surgeon's certificate of disability

Parker, William A.	Private	21	Sept. 20, 1861	3 yrs.

Transferred to Co. G, 8th O.V.C., Jan. 4, 1864; veteran

Penny, Beverly	Private	21	Sept. 20, 1861	3 yrs.

Transferred to Co. G, 8th O.V.C., Jan. 4, 1864; veteran

Power, James	Private	40	Sept. 20, 1861	3 yrs.

No further record found.

Rape, Lafayette	Private	19	Sept. 20, 1861	3 yrs.

Transferred to Co. G, 8th O.V.C., Jan. 4, 1864; veteran

Reck, John W.	Private	23	Sept. 20, 1861	3 yrs.

Transferred to Co. G, 8th O.V.C., Jan. 4, 1864; veteran

Renthler, Martin	Private	23	Sept. 20, 1861	3 yrs.

Discharged Jan. 8, 1863, at Lexington, Ky., on Surgeon's certificate of disability

Roger, Andrew	Private	21	Sept. 20, 1861	3 yrs.

Transferred to Co. G, 8th O.V.C., Jan. 4, 1864; veteran

Ross, Isaac M.	Private	20	Sept. 20, 1861	3 yrs.

Transferred to Co. G, 8th O.V.C., Jan. 4, 1864; veteran

Ross, Jacob I.	Private	19	Sept. 20, 1861	3 yrs.

Transferred to Co. G, 8th O.V.C., Jan. 4, 1864; veteran

Ross, Solomon H.	Private	20	Sept. 20, 1861	3 yrs.

Transferred to Co. G, 8th O.V.C., Jan. 4, 1864; veteran

Sackman, Asa	Private	22	Sept. 20, 1861	3 yrs.

Transferred to Co. G, 8th O.V.C., Jan. 4, 1864; veteran

44th REGIMENT OHIO VOLUNTEER INFANTRY *(Continued)*

Names	Rank	Age	Date of Entering the Service	Period of Service
Schemel, Thaddeus..........	Private	40	Sept. 20, 1861	3 yrs.
Transferred to Co. G, 8th O.V.C., Jan. 4, 1864; veteran				
Scribner, Franklin...........	Private	34	Sept. 20, 1861	3 yrs.
Transferred to Co. G, 8th O.V.C., Jan. 4, 1864; veteran				
Shields, Abraham............	Private	44	Sept. 20, 1861	3 yrs.
Discharged March 27, 1863, at Cincinnati, O., on Surgeon's certificate of disability				
Shields, George................	Private	23	Sept. 20, 1861	3 yrs.
Transferred to Co. G, 8th O.V.C., Jan. 4, 1864; veteran				
Shields, William................	Private	20	Sept. 20, 1861	3 yrs.
Transferred to Co. G, 8th O.V.C., Jan. 4, 1864; veteran				
Sutherland, Barnet..........	Private	23	Sept. 20, 1861	3 yrs.
Transferred to Co. G, 8th O.V.C., Jan. 4, 1864; veteran				
Swarthwood, Daniel...........	Private	19	Sept. 20, 1861	3 yrs.
Taylor, Clinton.................	Private	25	Sept. 20, 1861	3 yrs.
No further record found				
Taylor, Garrett.................	Private	18	Sept. 20, 1861	3 yrs.
Transferred to Co. G, 8th O.V.C., Jan. 4, 1864; veteran				
Taylor, Joshua...................	Private	19	Sept. 20, 1861	3 yrs.
Transferred to Co. G, 8th O.V.C., Jan. 4, 1864				
Taylor, Wesley M.............	Private	25	Sept. 20, 1861	3 yrs.
Discharged April 5, 1862, at Camp Piatt, W. Va., on Surgeon's certificate of disability				
Thompson, Robert............	Private	20	Sept. 20, 1861	3 yrs.
Transferred to Co. G, 8th O.V.C., Jan. 4, 1864; veteran				
Thorp, Tunis W.................	Private	19	Sept. 20, 1861	3 yrs.
Discharged Oct. 6, 1862, at Gallipolis, O., on Surgeon's certificate of disability				
Wickar, Alfred..................	Private	18	Sept. 20, 1861	3 yrs.
Transferred to Co. G, 8th O.V.C., Jan. 4, 1864; veteran				
Wickar, William...............	Private	18	Sept. 20, 1861	3 yrs.
Transferred to Co. G, 8th O.V.C., Jan. 4, 1864; veteran				
Winetland, Daniel...........	Private	26	Sept. 20, 1861	3 yrs.
Transferred to Co. G, 8th O.V.C., Jan. 4, 1864; veteran				
Wolf, Elihu......................	Private	30	Sept. 20, 1861	3 yrs.
Transferred to Co. G, 8th O.V.C., Jan. 4, 1864; veteran				

8th REGIMENT OHIO VOLUNTEER CAVALRY

Field and Staff

Mustered in from January - to April -, 1864, at Cincinnati, Ohio, by U.S. Mustering Officers. Mustered out July 30, 1865, at Clarksburg, W. Va., by Alphonzo Pettit, Captain 8th O.V.C., Acting Commissary of Musters, District of Clarksburg, W. Va.

Names	Rank	Age	Date of Entering the Service	Period of Service
Samuel A. Gilbert	Colonel	-	Oct. 14, 1861	3 yrs.
	Transferred from 44th O.V.I. Jan. 4, 1864; resigned April 20, 1864			
Alpheus S. Moore	Colonel	23	Aug. 31, 1861	3 yrs.
	Transferred from 44th O.V.I. as Major, Jan. 4, 1864; promoted to Lieut. Colonel, Jan. 30, 1864; to Colonel, May 9, 1864; honorably discharged Jan. 4, 1864			
Thomas Drummond	Colonel	-	Jan. 20, 1865	3 yrs.
	Promoted from Captain 5th U.S. Cavalry, Jan. 20, 1865, but not mustered; killed April 1, 1865, in battle of Five Forks, Va., while in command of the 5th U.S. Cavalry			
Wesley Owens	Colonel	32	May 2, 1865	3 yrs.
	Promoted from Captain 5th U.S. Cavalry; mustered out with regiment July 30, 1865			
Lysander W. Tulleys	Lt. Col.	26	Sept. 5, 1861	3 yrs.
	Transferred from 44th O.V.I. Jan. 4, 1864; honorably discharged Jan. 30, 1864			
Robert Youart	Lt. Col.	31	Aug. 31, 1861	3 yrs.
	Promoted to Major from Captain Co. L, Jan. 30, 1864; to Lieut. Colonel, May 9, 1864			
Augustus Dotze	Lt. Col.	31	Sept. 18, 1861	3 yrs.
	Promoted to Major from Captain Co. E, May, 1864; to Lieut. Colonel, May 31, 1865; mustered out with regiment July 30, 1865			
Jacob A. Souders	Major	22	Sept. 10, 1861	3 yrs.
	Promoted from Captain Co. H, May 9, 1864; honorably discharged May 29, 1865			
James W. Shaw	Major	22	Sept. 20, 1861	3 yrs.
	Promoted from Captain Co. G, May 9, 1864; mustered out with regiment, July 30, 1865			
Nicholas D. Badger	Major	25	Sept. 5, 1861	3 yrs.
	Promoted from Captain Co. C, Dec. 14, 1864; mustered out with regiment, July 30, 1865			
Henry K. Steele	Surgeon	36	Sept. 26, 1861	3 yrs.
	Transferred from 44th O.V.I., Jan. 4, 1864; mustered out Oct. 6, 1864, on expiration of term of service			
Milton J. Bowland	Surgeon	37	May 14, 1864	3 yrs.
	Promoted from Asst. Surgeon, Oct. 6, 1864; mustered out with regiment, July 30, 1865			

8th REGIMENT OHIO VOLUNTEER CAVALRY *(Continued)*

Names	Rank	Age	Date of Entering the Service	Period of Service
Benjamin F. Davis	As. Surg.	27	March 11 1863	3 yrs.

Transferred from 44th O.V.I. Jan. 4, 1864; mustered out with regiment, July 30, 1865

| Lewis H. Hazeltine | As. Surg. | 26 | May 11, 1865 | 3 yrs. |

Transferred from 44th O.V.I., Jan. 4, 1864; mustered out with regiment, July 30, 1865

| John G. Telford | Adjutant | 18 | Aug. 20, 1861 | 3 yrs. |

Transferred from 44th O.V.I., Jan. 4, 1864; promoted to Captain and Act. Adjt. General, Feb. 29, 1864

| Alphonso Pettit | Adjutant | 23 | Aug. 31, 1861 | 3 yrs. |

Appointed from 1st Lieutenant Co. L, April 11, 1864; promoted to Captain Co. L, May 9, 1864

| Thomas B. Burkholder | Adjutant | 18 | Sept. 5, 1861 | 3 yrs. |

Appointed from 1st Lieutenant Co. L, May 16, 1864; killed Sept. 18, 1864, in action at Martinsburg, W. Va.,; veteran

| Eli Kelly | Adjutant | 21 | Aug. 31, 1861 | 3 yrs. |

Appointed acting adjutant from 2d Lieutenant Co. L —; promoted to 1st Lieutenant, May 11, 1865, but not mustered; honorably discharged May 31, 1865; veteran

| James M. Kurtz | Adjutant | 21 | Oct. 9, 1861 | 3 yrs. |

Promoted to Sergt. Major from private Co. I, May 21, 1864; promoted to 1st Lieutenant Co. C, May 11, 1865; appointed from 1st Lieutenant Co. C, June 12, 1865; mustered out with regiment, July 30, 1865; veteran

| Warden M. Wheeler | R.Q.M. | 30 | May 9, 1864 | 3 yrs. |

Mustered out with regiment, July 30, 1865

| William W. Knoop | R.C.S. | 29 | Sept. 16, 1861 | 3 yrs. |

Transferred from 44th O.V.I. as 1st Lieutenant Co. F, Jan. 4, 1864; promoted to Captain, Jan. 30, 1864, but declined promotion; mustered out with regiment, July 30, 1865

| Edward Conner | Chaplain | 49 | June 9, 1864 | 3 yrs. |

Mustered out with regiment July 30, 1865

| Lafayette Bechtel | Ser. Maj. | 21 | Sept. 16, 1861 | 3 yrs. |

Transferred from 44th O.V.I., Jan. 4, 1864, promoted to 1st Lieutenant Co. I, Jan. 1864; veteran

| Wilmon W. Swain | Ser. Maj. | 19 | Sept. 16, 1861 | 3 yrs. |

Promoted from Sergeant Co. E —; to 1st Lieutenant Co. C, May 9, 1864; veteran

| Benjamin F. Crawford | Ser. Maj. | 18 | Aug. 31, 1861 | 3 yrs. |

Promoted from 1st Sergeant Co. A, May 21, 1865; mustered out with regiment, July 30, 1865; veteran

8th REGIMENT OHIO VOLUNTEER CAVALRY *(Continued)*

Names	Rank	Age	Date of Entering the Service	Period of Service
John B. Fagan	Q.M.S.	28	Sept. 16, 1861	3 yrs.

Transferred from 44th O.V.I., Jan. 4, 1864; mustered out with regiment, July 30, 1865; veteran

Joseph Pearson	Com. Ser.	24	Sept. 14, 1861	3 yrs.

Promoted from Sergeant Co. F —; mustered out with regiment, July 30, 1865; veteran

Silas F. Edgar	Hos. St'd	28	Oct. 10, 1861	3 yrs.

Transferred from 44th O.V.I., Jan. 4, 1864; mustered out with regiment, July 30, 1865; veteran

Albert H. Vance	Hos. St'd	28	Aug. 31, 1861	3 yrs.

Promoted from private Co. A, April 28, 1864; mustered out with regiment, July 30, 1865; veteran

Lyman Munger	Ch'f Bug.	19	Sept. 5, 1861	3 yrs.

Promoted from private Co. C —; reduced Jan. 28, 1865, at his own request, and assigned to Co. C; veteran

Aaron Miller	Ch'f Bug.	19	Sept. 10, 1861	3 yrs.

Promoted from Bugler Co. B, Jan. 28, 1865; mustered out with regiment, July 30, 1865; veteran

Philip Traebing	Sad. Ser.	39	March 16, 1864	3 yrs.

Promoted from private Co. L, April 1, 1864; mustered out with regiment, July 30, 1865

Company G.

Mustered in April 14, 1864, at Camp Dennison, Ohio, by A.F. Bond, Captain U.S.A. Mustering Officer. Mustered out July 30, 1865, at Clarksburg, W. Va., by Alphonzo Pettit, Captain 8th O.V.C., Acting Commissary of Musters, District of Clarksburg, W. Va.

James W. Shaw	Captain	22	Sept. 20, 1861	3 yrs.

Transferred from Co. G, 44th O.V.I., Jan. 4, 1864; promoted to Major, May 9, 1864

Alexander McAlpine	Captain	32	Sept. 20, 1861	3 yrs.

Transferred from Co. G, 44th O.V.I., as 2d Lieutenant, Jan. 4, 1864; promoted to 1st Lieutenant, April 25, 1864, to date Sept. 23, 1863; to Captain, May 9, 1864; mustered out with company, July 30, 1865

John H. Babb	1st Lieut.	23	Sept. 2, 1861	3 yrs.

Promoted from 2d Lieutenant Co. C, May 9, 1864; resigned June 13, 1865; veteran

8th REGIMENT OHIO VOLUNTEER CAVALRY *(Continued)*

Names	Rank	Age	Date of Entering the Service	Period of Service
George H. Potter	2d Lieut.	21	Sept. 20, 1861	3 yrs.

Transferred from Co. G, 44th O.V.I., as Sergeant, Jan. 4, 1864; promoted to 2d Lieutenant, May 9, 1864; to 1st Lieutenant Co. L, Nov. 12, 1864; veteran

Samuel J. Harrison	2d Lieut.	22	Sept. 20, 1861	3 yrs.

Transferred from Co. G, 44th O.V.I., as Corporal, Jan. 4, 1864; appointed Sergeant, Jan. 5, 1864; 1st Sergeant —; promoted to 2d Lieutenant, May 11, 1865; mustered out with company, July 30, 1865; veteran

William E. Kerlinger	1st Sergt.	26	Sept. 20, 1861	3 yrs.

Transferred from Co. G, 44th O.V.I., as Sergeant, Jan. 4, 1864; appointed 1st Sergeant, May 21, 1865; mustered out with company, July 30, 1865; veteran

John A. McKee	Q.M.S.	19	Sept. 20, 1861	3 yrs.

Transferred from Co. G, 44th O.V.I., as Corporal, Jan. 4, 1864; appointed Sergeant, Jan. 5, 1864; Q.M. Sergeant —; mustered out with company, July 30, 1865; veteran

William B. Galloway	Com. Ser.	20	Sept. 20, 1861	3 yrs.

Transferred from Co. G, 44th O.V.I., as Corporal, Jan. 4, 1864; appointed —; killed Oct. 29, 1864, in battle of Beverly, W. Va.; veteran

Jacob S. Ross	Com. Ser.	19	Sept. 20, 1861	3 yrs.

Transferred from Co. G, 44th O.V.I., as private, Jan. 4, 1864; appointed Corporal —; Sergeant, Nov. 1, 1864; Com. Sergeant —; mustered out with company, July 30, 1865; veteran

John Curtner	Sergeant	21	Sept. 20, 1861	3 yrs.

Transferred from Co. G, 44th O.V.I., as Corporal, Jan. 4, 1864; appointed Sergeant, April 12, 1864; discharged July 11, 1865, on Surgeon's certificate of disability; veteran

John E. Harrison	Sergeant	21	Sept. 20, 1861	3 yrs.

Transferred from Co. G, 44th O.V.I., as Corporal, Jan. 4, 1864; appointed Sergeant, Jan. 5, 1864; mustered out with company, July 30, 1865; veteran

William H. Robbins	Sergeant	25	Sept. 20, 1861	3 yrs.

Transferred from Co. G, 44th O.V.I., as Corporal, Jan. 4, 1864; appointed Sergeant, Jan. 5, 1864; mustered out with company, July 30, 1865; veteran

Jacob B. Brown	Sergeant	27	Sept. 19, 1861	3 yrs.

Transferred from Co. G, 44th O.V.I., as private, Jan. 4, 1864; appointed Sergeant, Jan. 5, 1864; mustered out with company, July 30, 1865; veteran

Silas P. Engle	Sergeant	19	Sept. 20, 1861	3 yrs.

Transferred from Co. G, 44th O.V.I., as private, Jan. 4, 1864; appointed Sergeant, July 12, 1865; mustered out with company, July 30, 1865; veteran

8th REGIMENT OHIO VOLUNTEER CAVALRY *(Continued)*

Names	Rank	Age	Date of Entering the Service	Period of Service
Samuel Bishop	Sergeant	18	Sept. 19, 1861	3 yrs.

Transferred from Co. G, 44th O.V.I., as private, Jan. 4, 1864; appointed Sergeant, July 12, 1865; mustered out with company, July 30, 1865; veteran

| John H. Friday | Corporal | 19 | Sept. 20, 1861 | 3 yrs. |

Transferred from Co. G, 44th O.V.I., as Corporal, Jan. 4, 1864; discharged, July 11, 1865, on Surgeon's certificate of disability; veteran

| Rufus G. Kent | Corporal | 34 | Sept. 20, 1861 | 3 yrs. |

Transferred from Co. G, 44th O.V.I., as Corporal, Jan. 4, 1864; died Feb. 22, 1864; veteran

| Scipio Myers | Corporal | 44 | Aug. 5, 1862 | 3 yrs. |

Transferred from Co. G, 44th O.V.I., Jan. 4, 1864; appointed —; mustered out to date, May 30, 1865, by order of War Department

| Isaac M. Ross | Corporal | 20 | Sept. 20, 1861 | 3 yrs. |

Transferred from Co. G, 44th O.V.I., as private, Jan. 4, 1864; appointed —; mustered out with company, July 30, 1865; veteran

| Samuel W. Bennett | Corporal | 19 | Sept. 19, 1861 | 3 yrs. |

Transferred from Co. G, 44th O.V.I., as private, Jan. 4, 1864; appointed —; mustered out with company, July 30, 1865; veteran

| William H. Granger | Corporal | 19 | Sept. 20, 1861 | 3 yrs. |

Transferred from Co. G, 44th O.V.I., as private, Jan. 4, 1864; appointed —; mustered out with company, July 30, 1865; veteran

| Joseph H. Corbin | Corporal | 18 | Sept. 20, 1861 | 3 yrs. |

Transferred from Co. G, 44th O.V.I., as private, Jan. 4, 1864; appointed —; mustered out with company, July 30, 1865; veteran

| Thomas M. Clark | Corporal | 21 | Sept. 20, 1861 | 3 yrs. |

Transferred from Co. G, 44th O.V.I., as private, Jan. 4, 1864; appointed May 21, 1865; mustered out with company, July 30, 1865; veteran

| Solomon H. Ross | Corporal | 20 | Sept. 20, 1861 | 3 yrs. |

Transferred from Co. G, 44th O.V.I., as private, Jan. 4, 1864; appointed May 21, 1865; mustered out with company, July 30, 1865; veteran

| Hiram Wickle | Corporal | 18 | Sept. 20, 1861 | 3 yrs. |

Transferred from Co. G, 44th O.V.I., as private, Jan. 4, 1864; appointed July 12, 1865; mustered out with company, July 30, 1865; veteran

| George Shields | Corporal | 23 | Sept. 20, 1861 | 3 yrs. |

Transferred from Co. G, 44th O.V.I., as private, Jan. 4, 1864; appointed July 12, 1865; mustered out with company, July 30, 1865; veteran

| Robert D. Felton | Bugler | 19 | Sept. 20, 1861 | 3 yrs. |

Transferred from Co. G, 44th O.V.I., as private, Jan. 4, 1864; appointed —; mustered out with company, July 30, 1865; veteran

8th REGIMENT OHIO VOLUNTEER CAVALRY *(Continued)*

Names	Rank	Age	Date of Entering the Service	Period of Service
Daniel Wineland	Bugler	26	Sept. 20, 1861	3 yrs.

Transferred from Co. G, 44th O.V.I., as private, Jan. 4, 1864; appointed —; mustered out with company, July 30, 1865; veteran

William Folkerth	Farrier	22	Sept. 20, 1861	3 yrs.

Transferred from Co. G, 44th O.V.I., as private, Jan. 4, 1864; appointed —; mustered out with company, July 30, 1865; veteran

Marquis L. Hall	Farrier	25	Sept. 20, 1861	3 yrs.

Transferred from Co. G, 44th O.V.I., as private, Jan. 4, 1864; appointed —; mustered out with company, July 30, 1865; veteran

Adams, Benjamin F.	Private	25	Sept. 7, 1861	3 yrs.

Transferred from Co. G, 44th O.V.I., as Corporal, Jan. 4, 1864; transferred to Co. M —

Adams, Charles	Private	19	Feb. 22, 1864	3 yrs.

Mustered out with company, July 30, 1865

Adam, Gilbert	Private	18	Feb. 16, 1864	3 yrs.

Mustered out with company, July 30, 1865

Alread, Isaac M.	Private	18	Feb. 23, 1864	3 yrs.

Mustered out with company, July 30, 1865

Arens, Granville M.	Private	19	Sept. 20, 1861	3 yrs.

Transferred from Co. G, 44th O.V.I., Jan. 4, 1864; mustered out with company, July 30, 1865; veteran

Arnett, Bartholomew	Private	27	Feb. 11, 1864	3 yrs.

Captured Sept. 5, 1864, near Martinsburg, W. Va.; mustered out June 20, 1865 at Camp Chase, O., by order of War Department

Barrack, John	Private	19	Aug. 4, 1862	3 yrs.

Transferred from 44th O.V.I., Jan. 4, 1864; mustered out to date, May 30, 1865, by order of War Department

Bates, Valentine	Private	28	March 15, 1865	3 yrs.

Mustered out with company, July 30, 1865

Bennett, David F.	Private	18	Aug. 4, 1862	3 yrs.

Transferred from 44th O.V.I., Jan. 4, 1865; mustered out to date May 30, 1865, by order of War Department

Benson, Elijah M.	Private	21	Sept. 19, 1861	3 yrs.

Transferred from Co. G, 44th O.V.I., Jan. 4, 1864; mustered out Nov. 10, 1864, at Columbus, O., on expiration of term of service

Bierly, Harvey H.	Private	18	Aug. 4, 1862	3 yrs.

Transferred from Co. G, 44th O.V.I., Jan. 4, 1864; mustered out to date May 30, 1865, by order of war Department

Bierly, Henry P.	Private	23	Aug. 4, 1862	3 yrs.

Transferred from Co. G, 44th O.V.I., Jan. 4, 1864; mustered out to date, May 30, 1865, by order of War Department

8th REGIMENT OHIO VOLUNTEER CAVALRY *(Continued)*

Names	Rank	Age	Date of Entering the Service	Period of Service
Bierly, William W.	Private	21	Aug. 4, 1862	3 yrs.

Transferred from Co. G, 44th O.V.I., Jan. 4, 1864; mustered out to date, May 30, 1865, by order of War Department

Burch, Samuel	Private	20	Feb. 23, 1864	3 yrs.

Mustered out with company, July 30, 1865.

Byers, Alanson	Private	19	Sept. 19, 1861	3 yrs.

Transferred from Co. G, 44th O.V.I., Jan. 4, 184; mustered out with company, July 30, 1865; veteran

Byers, Harvey A.	Private	21	Sept. 19, 1861	3 yrs.

Transferred from Co. G, 44th O.V.I., Jan. 4, 1864; died Oct. 31, 1864, of wounds received in action; veteran

Byers, Stephen	Private	28	Feb. 23, 1864	3 yrs.

Mustered out with company, July 30, 1865

Clymer, William A.	Private	19	Feb. 11, 1864	3 yrs.

Mustered out with company, July 30, 1865

Cochran, Samuel H.	Private	23	Aug. 4, 1862	3 yrs.

Transferred from 44th O.V.I., Jan. 4, 1864; mustered out, Oct. 6, 1865, at Columbus, O., on expiration of term of service

Conner, David O.	Private	21	Sept. 9, 1861	3 yrs.

Transferred from Co. G, 44th O.V.I, Jan. 4, 1864; mustered out, Oct. 6, 1865, at Columbus, O., on expiration of term of service

Conner, William	Private	19	Sept. 20, 1861	3 yrs.

Transferred from Co. G, 44th O.V.I., Jan. 4, 1864; died June 13, 1865, in hospital at Philadelphia, Pa.; veteran

Cooper, Asthton F.	Private	18	Feb. 22, 1864	3 yrs.

Mustered out with company, July 30, 1865

Cozat, John F.	Private	18	Feb. 23, 1864	3 yrs.

Transferred to Co. M —

Craig, David N.	Private	19	Sept. 9, 1861	3 yrs.

Captured Oct. 30, 1863, near Marysville, Tenn.; transferred from Co. G, 44th O.V.I., as Sergeant, Jan. 4, 1864; mustered out Jan. 25, 1865, at Columbus, O., on expiration of term of service

Craig, Francis M.	Private	18	Sept. 9, 1861	3 yrs.

Transferred from Co. G, 44th O.V.I., Jan. 4, 1864; transferred to Co. M —

Creeger, William H.	Private	19	Sept. 20, 1861	3 yrs.

Transferred from Co. G, 44th O.V.I., as Sergeant, Jan. 4, 1864; died July 13, 1864, at Harper's Ferry, Va., of wounds received in action; veteran

Crick, John	Private	19	Feb. 22, 1864	3 yrs.

Mustered out with company, July 30, 1865

8th REGIMENT OHIO VOLUNTEER CAVALRY *(Continued)*

Names	Rank	Age	Date of Entering the Service	Period of Service
Deeds, William	Private	20	Sept. 20, 1861	3 yrs.

Transferred from Co. G, 44th O.V.I., Jan. 4, 1864; discharged on July 11, 1865, on Surgeon's certificate of disability; veteran

Doty, Martin V.B.	Private	19	Aug. 3, 1862	3 yrs.

Transferred from 44th O.V.I., Jan. 4, 1864; mustered out to date, May 30, 1865, by order of War Department

Douglas, Grier	Private	18	Feb. 11, 1864	3 yrs.

Mustered out with company, July 30, 1865

Drishman, John	Private	31	Feb. 24, 1864	3 yrs.

Mustered out with company, July 30, 1865

Eirsman, Daniel	Private	21	Aug. 4, 1862	3 yrs.

Transferred from 44th O.V.I., Jan. 4, 1864; mustered out to date, May 30, 1865, by order of War Department

Elson, Albert	Private	18	Feb. 22, 1864	3 yrs.

Killed June 19, 1864, in action at Liberty, Va.

Falkner, David	Private	18	Oct. 28, 1862	3 yrs.

Transferred from 44th O.V.I., Jan. 4, 1864; transferred to Co. M —

Falkner, Jacob	Private	18	Oct. 28, 1862	3 yrs.

Transferred from 44th O.V.I., Jan. 4, 1864; to Co. F, 23d Regiment Veteran Reserve Corps, Oct. 14, 1863, from which mustered out as Corporal, Oct. 30, 1865, at Milwaukee, Wis., on expiration of term of service

Flemming, Charles	Private	21	Sept. 20, 1861	3 yrs.

Transferred from Co. G, 44th O.V.I., Jan. 4, 1864; mustered out with company, July 30, 1865; veteran

Folkerth, Jacob	Private	37	Aug. 4, 1862	3 yrs.

Transferred from 44th O.V.I., Jan. 4, 1864; mustered out to date, May 30, 1865, by order of War Department

Folkerth, Lorenzo D.	Private	22	Aug. 4, 1862	3 yrs.

Transferred from 44th O.V.I., Jan. 4, 1864; mustered out to date, May 30, 1865, by order of War Department

French, Walter W.	Private	18	Feb. 22, 1864	3 yrs.

Died Feb. 25, 1865, in hospital at Grafton, W. Va.

Fry, John	Private	19	Feb. 16, 1864	3 yrs.

Mustered out with company, July 30, 1865

Galloway, Joshua G.	Private	18	Sept. 20, 1861	3 yrs.

Transferred from Co. G, 44th O.V.I., Jan. 4, 1864; captured Jan. 11, 1865, at battle of Beverly, W. Va.; mustered out June 19, 1865, at Camp Chase, O., by order of War Department; veteran

Gower, Thomas B.	Private	24	Feb. 22, 1864	3 yrs.

Mustered out with company, July 30, 1865

8th REGIMENT OHIO VOLUNTEER CAVALRY *(Continued)*

Names	Rank	Age	Date of Entering the Service	Period of Service
Graham, John W.	Private	18	Sept. 20, 1861	3 yrs.
Transferred from Co. G, 44th O.V.I., Jan. 4, 1864; mustered out with company, July 30, 1865; veteran				
Hahn, Simon	Private	20	Feb. 25, 1864	3 yrs.
Mustered out with company, July 30, 1865				
Harper, Benjamin	Private	27	Sept. 20, 1861	3 yrs.
Transferred from Co. G, 44th O.V.I., Jan. 4, 1864; mustered out with company, July 30, 1865; veteran				
Harrison, Harvey A.	Private	22	Feb. 20, 1864	3 yrs.
Mustered out with company, July 30, 1865				
Hays, Samuel	Private	28	Aug. 31, 1864	1 yr.
Mustered out to date, May 30, 1865, by order of War Department				
Hecker, Albert M.	Private	20	Feb. 16, 1864	3 yrs.
Mustered out with company, July 30, 1865				
Hittenbrock, Henry	Private	-	Aug. 5, 1862	3 yrs.
Transferred from 44th O.V.I., Jan. 4, 1864; died Dec. 12, 1864, in prison at Charleston, South Carolina				
Horner, James M.	Private	23	Feb. 25, 1864	3 yrs.
Mustered out with company, July 30, 1865				
Huls, Henry	Private	22	Feb. 22, 1864	3 yrs.
Captured Jan. 11, 1865, in battle of Beverly, W. Va.; mustered out June 20, 1865, at Camp Chase, O., by order of War Department				
Hurley, Benjamin	Private	19	Sept. 20, 1861	3 yrs.
Transferred from Co. G, 44th O.V.I., Jan. 4, 1864; mustered out with company, July 30, 1865; veteran				
Inman, William M.	Private	34	Dec. 28, 1863	3 yrs.
Transferred from 44th O.V.I., Jan. 4, 1864; mustered out with company, July 30, 1865				
Johnson, Francis L.	Private	20	Sept. 9, 1861	3 yrs.
Transferred from Co. G, 44th O.V.I., Jan. 4, 1864; captured Jan. 11, 1865, at battle of Beverly, W. Va; mustered out June 30, 1865, at Camp Chase, O., by order of War Department				
Keihl, David A.	Private	25	Feb. 13, 1865	3 yrs.
Mustered out with company July 30, 1865				
Kenneke, Harman A.	Private	30	March 21, 1864	3 yrs.
Transferred to Co. M —				
Kessler, George	Private	19	Sept. 20, 1861	3 yrs.
Transferred from Co. G, 44th O.V.I., Jan. 4, 1864; died March 31, 1864; veteran				

8th REGIMENT OHIO VOLUNTEER CAVALRY *(Continued)*

Names	Rank	Age	Date of Entering the Service	Period of Service
Kiefer, Christian	Private	26	Sept. 20, 1861	3 yrs.

Transferred from Co. G, 44th O.V.I., Jan. 4, 1864

| Kindle, Thomas | Private | 28 | Aug. 20, 1862 | 3 yrs. |

Transferred from 44th O.V.I., Jan. 4, 1864; mustered out to date, May 30, 1865, by order of War Department

| Kring, Elijah | Private | 22 | Aug. 20, 1862 | 3 yrs. |

Transferred from 44th O.V.I., Jan. 4, 1864; mustered out to date May 30, 1865, by order of War Department

| Locker, David P. | Private | 18 | Feb. 23, 1864 | 3 yrs. |

Mustered out with company, July 30, 1865

| McCowen, Henry H. | Private | 39 | Aug. 5, 1862 | 3 yrs. |

Also born on rolls as "Henry H. McEuwan"; transferred from 44th O.V.I., Jan. 4, 1864; mustered out to date May 30, 1865, by order of War Department

| Martin, Jackson | Private | 23 | Aug. 5, 1862 | 3 yrs. |

Transferred from 44th O.V.I., Jan. 4, 1864; mustered out to date May 30, 1865, by order of War Department

| Martin, John R. | Private | 20 | Aug. 5, 1862 | 3 yrs. |

Transferred from 44th O.V.I., Jan. 4, 1864; killed June 15, 1864, in action near Liberty, Va.

| Martin, William A. | Private | 20 | Sept. 20, 1861 | 3 yrs. |

Transferred from Co. G, 44th O.V.I., as Corporal, Jan. 4, 1864; mustered out with company July 30, 1865; veteran

| Martin, William H. | Private | 23 | Feb. 18, 1864 | 3 yrs. |

Mustered out with company July 30, 1865

| Meeker, Rufus G. | Private | 19 | Sept. 20, 1861 | 3 yrs. |

Transferred from Co. G, 44th O.V.I., Jan. 4, 1864; discharged April 25, 1864, by order of War Department

| Miller, Benjamin | Private | 28 | Feb. 16, 1864 | 3 yrs. |

Mustered out with company July 30, 1865

| Moldin, Joseph | Private | 23 | Feb. 23, 1864 | 3 yrs. |

Also borne on rolls as "Joseph Modlin"; mustered out with company July 30, 1865

| Morrison, Robert A. | Private | 32 | Feb. 25, 1864 | 3 yrs. |

Mustered out with company July 30, 1865

| Mote, Irwin | Private | 31 | Sept. 20, 1861 | 3 yrs. |

Transferred from Co. G, 44th O.V.I., Jan. 4, 1864; mustered out with company July 30, 1865; veteran

| Olwine, John | Private | 23 | Aug. 5, 1862 | 3 yrs. |

Transferred from Co. G, 44th O.V.I., Jan. 4. 1864; to Co. C, 104th O.V.I., Jan. 7, 1864

8th REGIMENT OHIO VOLUNTEER CAVALRY *(Continued)*

Names	Rank	Age	Date of Entering the Service	Period of Service
Overman, William	Private	23	Oct. 28, 1862	3 yrs.

Transferred from 44th O.V.I., Jan. 4, 1864; discharged Aug 29, 1863, as of Co. G, 44th O.V.I., on Surgeon's certificate of disability

| Parker, William A. | Private | 21 | Sept. 9, 1861 | 3 yrs. |

Transferred from Co. G, 44th O.V.I., Jan. 4, 1864; to Co. M —

| Penny, Beverly | Private | 21 | Sept. 20, 1861 | 3 yrs. |

Transferred from Co. G, 44th O.V.I., Jan. 4, 1864; captured Jan. 11, 1865, at battle of Beverly, W. Va.; mustered out June 19, 1865, at Camp Chase, O., by order of War Department; veteran

| Penny, Mercer | Private | 30 | March 20, 1865 | 1 yr. |

Mustered out with company July 30, 1865

| Polly, Joseph W. | Private | 18 | Feb. 17, 1864 | 3 yrs. |

Mustered out with company July 30, 1865

| Porter, Joseph K. | Private | 24 | Feb. 16, 1864 | 3 yrs. |

Also borne on rolls as "Jacob K."; captured Jan. 11, 1865, at battle of Beverly, W. Va.; mustered out June 19, 1865, at Camp Chase, O., by order of War Department

| Rape, Lafayette | Private | 19 | Sept. 9, 1861 | 3 yrs. |

Transferred from Co. G, 44th O.V.I., Jan. 4, 1864; to Co. E, 2d Regiment Veteran Reserve Corps, Oct. 1, 1863, from which mustered out Sept. 26, 1864, on expiration of term of service

| Reck, Elias O. | Private | 23 | Feb. 27, 1864 | 3 yrs. |

Mustered out with company July 30, 1865

| Reck, John W. | Private | 23 | Sept. 20, 1861 | 3 yrs. |

Transferred from Co. G, 44th O.V.I., Jan. 4, 1864; mustered out with company July 30, 1865; veteran

| Reed, Samuel F. | Private | 26 | Sept. 20, 1861 | 3 yrs. |

Transferred from Co. G, 44th O.V.I., as Corporal, Jan. 4, 1864; mustered out with company July 30, 1865; veteran

| Reedy, Christian | Private | 19 | Aug. 11, 1862 | 3 yrs. |

Transferred from 44th O.V.I., Jan. 4, 1864; died Jan. 16, 1864

| Renthler, Frederick | Private | 18 | Feb. 20, 1864 | 3 yrs. |

Also borne on rolls as "Rentchler"; mustered out with company July 30, 1865

| Renthler, Gottlieb | Private | 18 | Feb. 20, 1863 | 3 yrs. |

Also borne on rolls as "Rentchler"; mustered out May 27, 1865, at Gallipolis, O., by order of War Department

| Robbins, Moses H. | Private | 18 | Feb. 12, 1864 | 3 yrs. |

Mustered out with company July 30, 1865

8th REGIMENT OHIO VOLUNTEER CAVALRY *(Continued)*

Names	Rank	Age	Date of Entering the Service	Period of Service
Rogers, Andrew...............	Private	18	Sept. 20, 1861	3 yrs.

Transferred from Co. G, 44th O.V.I., Jan. 4, 1864; discharged April 30, 1865, on Surgeon's certificate of disability; veteran

| Sackman, Asa................... | Private | 22 | Sept. 20, 1861 | 3 yrs. |

Transferred from Co. G, 44th O.V.I., Jan. 4, 1864; killed Oct. 29, 1864, in battle of Beverly, W. Va.; veteran

| Schemel, Thaddeus......... | Private | 40 | Sept. 9, 1861 | 3 yrs. |

Transferred from Co. G, 44th O.V.I., Jan. 4, 1864; captured Sept. 11, 1863, in action at Gauley Bridge Ferry, W. Va.; mustered out Nov. 6, 1864, at Columbus, O., on expiration of term of service.

| Scribner, Franklin.......... | Private | 23 | Sept. 9, 1861 | 3 yrs. |

Transferred from Co. G, 44th O.V.I., Jan. 4, 1864; discharged April 9, 1864, by order of War Department

| Shields, William............... | Private | 20 | Sept. 20, 1861 | 3 yrs. |

Transferred from Co. G, 44th O.V.I., Jan. 4, 1864; mustered out with company July 30, 1865; veteran

| Silber, John...................... | Private | 24 | Aug. 11, 1862 | 3 yrs. |

Transferred from 44th O.V.I., Jan. 4, 1864; died March 3, 1864

| Smith, Henry................... | Private | 18 | Feb. 16, 1864 | 3 yrs. |

Mustered out with company, July 30, 1865

| Snider, Henry C. .... | Private | 18 | Jan. 27, 1864 | 3 yrs. |

Mustered out with company July 30, 1865

| Snouse, John.................... | Private | 20 | Aug. 11, 1862 | 3 yrs. |

Transferred from 44th O.V.I., Jan. 4, 1864; to Co. D. 23d Regiment Veteran Reserve Corps, Aug. 26, 1864, from which discharged Feb. 15, 1865, at Jeffersonville, Ind., on Surgeon's certificate of disability

| Stahl, Samuel................... | Private | 18 | Feb. 22, 1864 | 3 yrs. |

Captured Sept. 1, 1864, near Martinsburg, W. Va.; paroled prisoner of war at Camp Chase, O.; no further record found

| Sutherland, Barnett .... | Private | 23 | Sept. 9, 1861 | 3 yrs. |

Transferred from Co. G, 44th O.V.I., Jan. 4, 1864; died Jan. 17, 1864

| Swain, David F. .... | Private | 18 | Feb. 20, 1864 | 3 yrs. |

Mustered out with company July 30, 1865

| Tate, William H. .... | Private | 21 | Sept. 19, 1861 | 3 yrs. |

Transferred from Co. G, 44th O.V.I., as 1st Sergeant, Jan. 4, 1864; mustered out Sept. 30, 1864, at Columbus, O., on expiration of term of service as of Co. G, 44th O.V.I.

| Taylor, Garnett................ | Private | 18 | Sept. 20, 1861 | 3 yrs. |

Transferred from Co. G, 44th O.V.I., Jan. 4, 1864; captured Jan. 11, 1865, at battle of Beverly, W. Va.; mustered out July 3, 1865, at Camp Chase, O., by order of War Department; veteran

8th REGIMENT OHIO VOLUNTEER CAVALRY *(Continued)*

Names	Rank	Age	Date of Entering the Service	Period of Service
Taylor, Joshua	Private	21	Feb. 22, 1864	3 yrs.

Died March 24, 1864, at Versailles, O.

Teagarden, William Y.	Private	20	Feb. 10, 1864	3 yrs.

Mustered out with company July 30, 1865

Thomas, David R.	Private	24	Feb. 18, 1864	3 yrs.

Mustered out with company July 30, 1865

Thompson, Robert	Private	20	Sept. 21, 1861	3 yrs.

Transferred from Co. G, 44th O.V.I., Jan. 4, 1864; captured Jan. 11, 1865, at battle of Beverly, W. Va.; mustered out June 13, 1865, at Camp Chase, O., by order of War Department; veteran

Tomlinson, Edwin	Private	18	Feb. 11, 1864	3 yrs.

Mustered out with company July 30, 1865

Trowridge, Simon	Private	19	Feb. 23, 1864	3 yrs.

Mustered out with company July 30, 1865

Ullery, David	Private	18	Aug. 11, 1862	3 yrs.

Transferred from 44th O.V.I., Jan. 4, 1864; died Nov. 11, 1864, at Greenville, O.

Vantilburg, William	Private	19	Feb. 11, 1864	3 yrs.

Mustered out with company July 30, 1865

Wiekle, Alfred	Private	19	Feb. 23, 1865	3 yrs.

Mustered out with company July 30, 1865

Williamson, Emanuel	Private	32	Feb. 22, 1864	3 yrs.

Mustered out with company July 30, 1865

Wilson, Ira M.	Private	18	Feb. 20, 1864	3 yrs.

Mustered out with company July 30, 1865

Wolf, Elihu	Private	30	Sept. 9, 1861	3 yrs.

Transferred from Co. G, 44th O.V.I., Jan. 4, 1864; mustered out Sept. 20, 1864, at Columbus, O., on expiration of term of service, as of Co. G, 44th O.V.I.

Yager, Joseph C.	Private	18	Feb. 16, 1864	3 yrs.

Transferred to Co. H —

Young, James F.	Private	18	Feb. 16, 1864	3 yrs.

Mustered out with company July 30, 1865

INDEX

Adam, Gilbert 138
Alspaugh, Henry 35
Allegheny Mountains 38
Annapolis, Md 141
Antietam, Md 123
Antietam Campaign 50
Arcanum, Oh 110
Arens, Granville M. 110, 138
Averell, William W. 104, 105, 107, 110, 112, 128
Averell's Division 123

Babb, John H. 124, 127
Badger, Captain 73
Baird, Absalom 64
Baltimore & Ohio Railroad 5
Band, Regimental 109
Barboursville, Ky 72
Bardstown, Ky 57
Barrack, John 91, 138, 151
Beck, Michael 13
Bell, Capt. 10
Bell, John 51
Bellaire, Oh 144
Belle, WVa 11
Benham, G. W. 9
Bennett, Samuel 110
Berryville, Va 119
Beverly, WVa 23, 129, 132, 137, 139, 140, 144, 152
Bierly, Harvey 54, 138
Bierly, Henry 138, 151
Bierly, William W. 151
Big Springs 124
Bishop, Samuel 110, 138
Blue Sulphur Springs 45
Blowing Cave, Va 113
Botsford, J. L. 139
Bragg, Braxton 52, 82
Breckinridge, John C. 115
Brown, Jacob 12
Brough, John 68, 93, 101, 102
Buchanan 113, 115
Buckhannon, WVa 137
Bunker, Hill 119, 125 et. seq.
Burnside, Ambrose 68, 75, 79, 85
Butters, Major 140
Byers, Alanson 138
Byers, Harvey 129
Byers, Stephen 138

Campbell, Miss 152
Camp Chase, Oh 141, 155
Camp Clark, Oh 4
Camp Dennison, Oh 4, 13, 95, 96, 98, 159
Camp Dick Robinson, Ky 75, 77
Camp Enyart, WVa 5, 6, 8
Camp Nelson, Ky 86, 93
Camp Piatt, WVa 9, 11, 12, 13, 14, 16, 17, 21, 22, 24, 25, 27, 28
Cannelton, WVa 8
Carnifix Ferry, WVa 48
Catawba Mountain 114
Cedar Creek, Va 119
Chambersburg, Pa 120, 147
Charleston, WVa 98, 99, 101, 111
Chattanooga, Tn 79
Chicago Democratic Convention 124, 127
Childs, Chaplain Thomas P. 8, 10
"The Chimney Corner" 154
Cincinnati, Oh 159
Clarksburg, WVa 139, 141, 147, 150, 151, 159, 156, 157, 159
Clarkson, John N. 7
Clay, Henry 51
Clear Springs, Va 120
Clifton, WVa 8
Clinton, Mo 161
Columbus, Oh 151
Coots, Lemira Elliott 161
Corbin, Joseph H. 138
Covington, Ky 33, 51, 52, 54
Cox, Jacob D. 41
Crab Orchard, Ky 70, 71, 76
Creeger, William H. 27, 117, 118
Creigh, David S. 107, 112
Crick, John 111, 138
Criley, Alfred H. 112, et seq.
Crisis, The 103
Criswell, Capt. 148
Crook, George 29, 46, 104, 107, 113, 134, 138, 141
Cross Lanes, WVa 48
Cumberland, Va 120
Cumberland Gap 72, 79, 81
Cummings, Margaret — Foreword

Dalton, David 138
Danville, Ky 57, 71

Darke County, Oh 3
Darkesville, WVa 119
Davis, Jefferson 69
Dotze, Augustus 144, 159
Dennison, Gov. William 3
Derchen, Aaron 22
Draft Laws 47
Drischman, John 138, 146
Dry Run, Va 119
Duval, Isaac Hardin 140

Early, Jubal 115, 123
Eirsman, Daniel 54, 137
Election of 1864, 128
Elimore, Joseph 4
Elizabeth, Ky 57
Elson, Albert 110
Enfield Rifles 5, 22
Evans, Charles H. 138

Fayetteville, Va 120
Fisher's Hill, Va 119
Flemming, Charles 15, 138
Floyd, John B. 9, 10, 11
Folkerth, Jacob 138
Forest Hill, Va 119
Fort Donelson, Tn 51
Foster, John 93
Frankfort, Ky 63, 64, 65, 66
Friday, John 110
Furney, Lt. Col. 140, 141

Galloway, William B. 23, 129
Galloway, Joshua G. 138
Garret, Daniel 39
Gauley Bridge, WVa 9, 29, 30, 31, 32,
 50, 103, 105, 120
Gauley River 7
George, William 99
Georgetown, Ky 53
Gettysburg, Oh 3, 144
Gilbert, Cass 103
Gilbert, Charles Champion 103
Gilbert, Levi 17
Gilbert, Samuel Augustus 3, 14, 35, 44,
 51, 56, 67, 77, 88, 93, 94, 99, 101, 102,
 132, picture, p. 100
Gillmore, Q. A. 54
Gower, Thomas B. 138
Graham, John W. 76, 138
Granger, Gordon 51, 54
Granger, William H. 138

Greenbrier River 43
Greenville, Oh 3
Greenville Democrat 6
Greenwood Rifles 5, 6

Hagerstown, Md 119, 120, 123, 128, 129
Hahn, Simon 138
Hall, Marquis L. 138, 139
Hamilton, James
Hancock, Md 119, 120
Harman, Abe 12
Harper, Benjamin 138
Harpers Ferry, WVa 123, 129
Harrison, John E. 138
Harrison, Samuel 110, 138
Hartsuff, George L. 76
Hawks Nest 47, 112
Hayes, William 16
Hays, Calvin 40
Hays, Samuel 138
Hecker, Albert M. 125
Heth, Gen. Henry H. 33
Hickman's Bridge 75, 77, 130
Hill, Major 130
Hillsgrove, Oh 147
Horner, William A. 27, 120
Horner, James M. 111, 120, 138
Hot Springs 112
Houston, G. L. 44
Howendobler, Frank 147
Huls, Henry 138
Hunter, David 101, 107, 111, 112, 115, 132
Hurley, Benjamin 138, 156

Inman, William 138

Jackson Station 33
Jackson, Stonewall 113
James River 105
Jenkins, Col. A. G. 10
Johnson, Andrew 3, 4
Johnson, Francis L. 138
Judah, Henry M. 54

Kanawha River 5, 7, 29, 39, 67
Keefauver, Isaac 104
Keel, David 147
Kent, Rufus 53
Kentucky 51
Ky First Regiment 73
Kentucky River 56
Kerlinger, William E. 110

Kire, David 110
Knoxville, Tn 74, 79, 82, Siege 84 et seq.
Kring, Elijah 138

Lancaster, Ky 70
Langston, 13, 35
Langston, Len 110
Lebanon, Ky 57
Lee, Robert E. 115, 145
Letcher, John 107
Lewisburg Cannon 34
Lewisburg, WVa 32, 33, 36, 105, 111, 125, 145
Leestown, Va 125
Lexington, Ky 52, 53, 54, 57, 70, 107, 105
Liberty, Va 114
Lightburn, Joseph 59, 70
Lincoln, Abraham 3, death 146
Little Miami Railroad 3, 5
Locker, David P. 138
London, Ky 73, 77
Longstreet, James 83
Loring, W. W. 50
Louisville, Ky 51
Louisville & Nashville Rld. 57
Lynchburg Raid 105 et seq.
Lynchburg, Va 105, 113, 119, 147

Malden, WVa 17
Martin, Jack 82
Martin, John R. 110
Martin, William A. 138
Maus, Charles 23
Martinsburg, WVa 105, 111, 115, 119, 120, 123, 125, 128
McAlpine, Alexander 101, 138
McCausland, John 113, 116
McClellan, George B. 5, 81, 124, 128
McConnelsburg, Va 119, 120
MCCowen, Henry 124, 125, 138
McGrew, W. A. 155
McKee, Elizabeth 161
McKee, James T. 161
McKee, John, Death of 161
McKee, Lemira Elliot Coots 161
McKee, Margaret, Foreword, 161
McKee, Mary Frances Rickets 161
McKee, Sarah Jane Harper, Foreword,161
McKee, Susan, 161
McKee, Washington Joseph, Foreword, 161

Meadow Bluffs, WVa 36, 37, 39, 41, 45, 104, 111
Mercer County, Ohio 110
Milford, Va 119
Miller, Confederate Colonel 25
Mitchell, Ackber 59
Moldin, Joseph 138
Moore, Alpheus S. 72, 74, 87, 101, 132 et seq., resignation 134
Moore's Poetical Works 145
Moorefield, WVa 121
Morgan, John Hunt 52, 53, 57, 58, 76
Morrison, Robert A. 111
Mote, Irwin 138
Mount Jackson, Va 119
Mount Vernon, Ky 70, 74
Myers, Scipio 17, 55, 79, 117, 124, 138

Natural Bridge, Va 113
Newcreek, Va 119, 120
New Harrison 8
Newkirk, John M. 37, 54, 65
New River 29
Nenevah, Va 119
Ninth Virginia Regt. 43
North Shenadoah, Va 119

Ohio 18th Battery 56
Ohio 34th Regt. 139, 142
Ohio 47th Regt. 31
Ohio 152nd Regt. 105
Ohio 157th Regt. 105
Olwine, John 82
Orr, Capt. Tom 22, 105

Paducah, Ky 51
Palimer, Samuel 99
Paris, Ky 70
Parkersburg, WVa 115, 117, 119
Parole Camp 141
Peaks of Otter, Va 113
Pa. 14th Cav. 108, 113
Penny, Beverly 46, 138
Pettit, Alphonso 138
Phillippi 142, 144, 152
Piatt's Zouave Regt 5
Platona, WVa 10
Pleasant Valley, Md 129, 130, 134
Point Pleasant, Ky 52
Pope, General 46
Porter, Joseph K. 138
Port Republic, Va 104, 119

Potomac River 123
Potter, Gen. E. E. 88
Potter, George 138
Powell, W. H. 132, 133
Prisoners Paroled 141

Reck, Elias O. 138
Reck, John 35
Renthler, Frederick 138
Richland, Ks 161
Richmond, Ky 55, 69, 77
Richmond, Va 141
Rickets, Mary Frances 161
Robbins, William H. 138
Romney, WVa 121
Rosecrans, William 64, 82
Ross, Isaac 110, 138
Ross, Jacob S. 138
Ross, Solomon H. 138
Rosser, Thomas 138

Sackman, Asa 129, 130
Salem, Va 114
Sanders, William P. 75
Seiber, Col. 58
Sewell Mountain 33
Sharpsburg, Md 123
Shaw, James W. 64, 101, 142
Shepherdstown, Va 123
Sheridan, Philip 123, 128, 132, 141
Shields, Abe 22
Shields, George 138
Slavery 42
Smith, Henry 138
Smith, Kirby 52
Smithland, Ky 51
Snider, Henry 138
Souders, Jacob A. 140
Springfield Evening News 4
Springfield, Ohio 3
Springfield Republic 3, 10, 13, 57, 68
Springfield, WVa 121
Stahl, Samuel 155
Stanford, Ky 75, 77
Staunton, Va 104, 105, 115
Stough, Capt. 40
Stute, Henry K. 14
Swain, David F. 110
Swarthwood, Daniel 13
Sweet Springs 114

Tate, William H. 27

Taylor, Garnett 138
Taylor, Joshua 138
Teagarden, William 138
Tennessee (East) Cavalry 86
Tennessee, Raid into 74, 75
Thompson, Anson N. 86
Thompson, Robert 138
Thurmond's Rangers 46
Timberline, Va 119
Tomlinson, Edwin 144
Tompkins Farm 50 112
Tompkinsville, Ky 57
Topeka, Ks 161
Torbert, Alfred 130
Trowbridge, Simon 125, 138

Union, WVa 38
Union City, In 161

Vallandingham, Clement L. 66, 68
Virginia 1st Cavalry 120
Virginia 8th Cavalry 46
Virginia 11th Infantry 128
Virginia 22nd Infantry 46
Virginia 62nd Infantry 130

Warm Springs, WVa 151
Washington's Birthday 24
Webster, WVa 144
Weston, WVa 144, 145, 146, 147, 150, 154
West Va., Army of 118 et seq.
Western Virginia 5
White, Rev. 4
White Sulphur Springs, WVa 32, 112
Wilcox, James A. 96
Wiekle, Alfred 138
Wiekle, William 138
Wild Cat, Ky 77
Wilkinson, Nathan 138, 141
Williamsport, Md 120, 123
Williamsport, Pa 119
Winchester, Va 119, 124
Wilson, H. Blair 4, 10, 23, 74,
Wilson, Ira M. 138
Windy Cove Gap 113

Xenia, Oh 96

Young, James 110
Youart, Robert 133, 139, 141, 143

Zimmerman, Abe 22